GIFT WRAPPING

GIFT

WRAPPING
Creative Ideas from Japan

Kunio Ekiguchi

photographed by
Akihiko Tokue

KODANSHA INTERNATIONAL LTD.
Tokyo and New York

The original instructions for each gift wrapping were prepared by Michiko Itō.

The introduction and the sections on Mizuhiki (p. 68), Layering and Color (p. 88), and Furoshiki (p. 113) were translated by Stephen B. Snyder.

Drawings by Eiko Ikeda.

The publisher would like to thank the following for supplying goods: Matsuya Department Store for the wine on the front jacket, the jam on pages 36 and 37 (Gifts 18, 19), the baby shoes on page 89 (Gift 45), the baby clothes on page 89 (Gift 46), the necktie on page 92 (Gift 55), and the gloves on page 92 (Gift 56); Minobe Co., Ltd. for the *furoshiki* on pages 111 (Gift 60) and 112 (Gift 64); and Yamada Heiandō for the lacquer box on page 9 (Gift 3).

Distributed in the United States by Kodansha International/USA Ltd. through Harper & Row, Publishers, Inc., 10 East 53rd Street, New York, New York 10022.

Published by Kodansha International Ltd., 2-2, Otowa 1-chome, Bunkyo-ku, Tokyo 112 and Kodansha International/USA Ltd., 10 East 53rd Street, New York, New York 10022.

Library of Congress Cataloging in Publication Data
Ekiguchi, Kunio, 1930–
    Gift wrapping.
    1. Gift wrapping. I. Title
TT870.E375 1985 745.54 85–40058
ISBN 0-87011-768-8
ISBN 4-7700-1268-3 (in Japan)

CONTENTS

Introduction

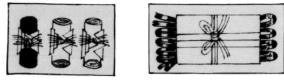

In Japan, the concept of wrapping, tsutsumi, *is not limited to the function of packaging. It plays a central role in a wide variety of spiritual and cultural aspects of Japanese life.* Tsutsumi *encompasses many areas not included in the Western concept of wrapping. For example, gods or Buddhas are "wrapped" in a household altar containing a hidden image of the god or a portable shrine carried during festivals; gardens are enclosed by a variety of fences; architectural space is defined by translucent* shoji *doors, opaque* fusuma *doors, and bamboo blinds; pictures are rolled up in hanging scrolls and picture scrolls; and food is placed in lacquer containers. The wrapping style illustrated by these examples is not a tight, hermetic seal, but a loose, flexible covering or shading. This style embodies the concept of "gentle concealment," a central part of the traditional Japanese sense of beauty.*

The word tsutsumi *is thought to come from the verb* tsutsushimu, *"to refrain, to be discreet or moderate." The Japanese spirit tends to shun things that are direct, blunt, or frank and favors those which are controlled, indirect, and restrained. Restraint has come to be synonymous with refinement, and this value is in turn reflected in all segments of Japanese cultural life; the elegant, minimal—yet expressive—movements of Nō; the simplicity of black ink paintings; and the unpainted and unadorned surfaces of Japanese architecture illuminated with the light filtering through* shoji *doors.*

The tsutsushimu *aesthetic also plays an important role in gift giving. The Japanese have always considered it discourteous simply to pass an unwrapped, unconcealed object from one hand to another. The object was wrapped in white* washi *(Japanese paper), or, if it could not be wrapped, paper was spread over or under it. Wrapping in paper became analogous to a kind of pledge that the contents were protected from all impurities. The fact that* washi, *once creased, will hold the crease forever has also come to symbolize this seal against impurities.*

White paper is used because white is the color of the gods and, therefore, is free of all contamination. A newborn baby, for example, is considered to be a god and is dressed in white clothing. When it is seventeen days old, the white robe is changed for a colorful one, and only then is the baby considered a human child. Similarly, a bride is dressed in a white kimono during the wedding ceremony, signifying that she is first a bride of the gods. After the ceremony, she changes to a brilliantly colored kimono to indicate that she has become the bride of a human. In the same way, the bodies of the dead are wrapped in sacred white to prepare them for the return to the gods.

Building on this long and rich tradition of wrapping in white, the art of gift wrapping, origata, *was developed.* Origata *is governed by a complex set of rules that determine the style of wrapping according to such factors as the recipient of the gift, the gift itself, and the occasion.*

There are special terms and special rules for wrapping certain items: kinsu-zutsumi, *wrapping gifts of money;* fude-zutsumi, *wrapping brushes;* suzuri-zutsumi, *wrapping ink stones;* hashi-tsutsumi, *wrapping chopsticks;* gofuku-tsutsumi, *wrapping kimono;* obi-tsutsumi, *wrapping kimono sashes;* ōgi-tsutsumi, *wrapping fans;* oshiroi-tsutsumi, *wrapping facial powder;* kushi-zutsumi, *wrapping combs;* beni-tsutsumi, *wrapping*

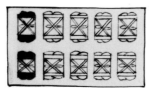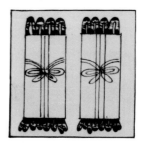

rouge; hari-tsutsumi, *wrapping needles*; kō-zutsumi, *wrapping incense—and so on indefinitely.*

The style or materials for wrapping vary according to the occasion as well. There are special wrappings for congratulatory gifts, for going-away presents, for presents taken to the sick, for offerings to the gods, and for funeral gifts. In fact, it is difficult to say how many different kinds of origata *exist. What is more, within each variety other factors, such as the relationship between the giver and the receiver and the season in which the gift is given also must be taken into consideration when selecting the paper,* mizuhiki *cords, and style of wrapping. With the exceptions of formal occasions such as funerals and weddings, however, many of the more complex forms of* origata *have fallen into disuse. Nonetheless, they continue to be practiced even today among people who still value the finer points of courtesy and consideration.*

In Japan, it is said that giving a gift is like wrapping one's heart. Just as one helps a friend into a coat carefully and courteously, a gift should be wrapped tenderly and conscientiously. While the wrapping should, of course, protect the contents from breakage or other damage, the same care should be taken with aspects normally thought of as merely decorative—those that reflect the sentiment of the giver—the paper and the way it is wrapped, the ribbon and the way it is tied. This need not entail expensive, ostentatious materials. Innovative and elegant packages can be created using the materials on hand and a few basic Japanese wrapping concepts. In this book I have used paper and cloth as the basic wrapping materials, but tsutsumi *also makes use of natural materials such as leaves, leather, bamboo, bamboo grass, straw, and so on. This ingenuity is especially apparent in the packaging of sweets and other foods. One of the secrets of such wrappings is to simply overcome the idea that paper is the only possibility. Creative alternatives should be sought with a flexible, imaginative eye.*

In Japan, the changing of the seasons is a particularly central aspect of life, and this too plays a role in tsutsumi *aesthetics. There are two major gift-giving seasons in Japan today. One is from late June to early July (o-chūgen) and the other at year's end (o-seibo). The gifts are wrapped to complement the season, with coolness and lightness the theme for the summer gifts and warm motifs for the winter. This seasonal consciousness need not be limited to summer and winter, but can be used to add interest to a gift at any time of the year. In early spring, evoke the scent of the first blossoms by cutting flower petals out of colorful paper and pressing them between thin sheets of translucent wrapping paper. Red and gold leaves tucked under a ribbon capture an autumn mood.*

This book is intended to provide a basis from which to invent your own personalized wrappings—ones that express your feelings and creativity. I hope some of the ideas found herein will be helpful.

I would like to take this opportunity to thank my assistants Michiko Itō and Kazutoshi Omoda for their patience and diligence and also Michiko Uchiyama and Rowena Wildin, my editors at Kodansha International.

Before You Begin

FIRST THINGS FIRST

Gift wrapping is different from paper craft and other creative activities in that the wrapping is not an end—it is the means by which to convey the love and thought that go into the giving of a gift. Therefore, the size, shape, and very nature of the wrapping are determined by the gift itself, the occasion, and the personalities of the people giving and receiving the gift.

The sixty-six gift wrappings in this book have been divided into basic shapes and types to make it easier for you to find the right one for your present. So begin by taking a good look at the shape and size of your gift. Find a similarly shaped wrapping and make it smaller or larger as needed.

Gift wrapping is easy and rewarding, and you will be surprised to find that many of the very elaborate-looking ideas are really very simple. Follow the steps below for perfect-every-time results.

1. Read through the instructions once.

2. Decide what to wrap the gift in. Would a box be better or can the shape of the gift itself be used? Will you use cloth or paper, ribbon, mizuhiki, or something else? Experiment with color and prints.

Mix papers and textures. And make sure you have scissors, glue, tape, double-faced tape, a compass, wire, string, or whatever other materials may be necessary.

3. Practice with scrap paper or any inexpensive paper of about the same weight as the paper you plan to use. If you still have trouble understanding how to fold the wrapping, try practicing with a sheet of paper about the same size as that given in the instructions.

4. Adjust the size given in the instructions to fit your box. Measurements have been given as exactly as possible to give you an idea of the relationship between gift size and wrapping size. All dimensions are given in inches. For those who are more comfortable working in centimeters, convert inches to centimeters by multiplying the number of inches by 2.5. (To convert centimeters to inches, multiply the number of centimeters by 0.4.)

5. Wrap your gift according to the step-by-step instructions and add any finishing touches like ribbon, mizuhiki, stickers, etc.

PAPER AND OTHER MATERIALS

Gift wrapping paper is available in a wide range of prints, colors, and metallics, and sold in stationery stores, card shops, art supply stores, department stores, and so on. But do not limit yourself to gift wrapping paper: try using the different types of paper around you—pages from magazines, paper doilies, posters, cellophane, crepe paper, etc. Or try washi, handmade Japanese paper. Washi is available in a variety of weights and types. Its durability, flexibility, and soft lustrousness make it a natural for soft, boxless wrappings. Washi is available at oriental import stores and some art stores (see Appendix, page 123). Or forget paper and use cloth—furoshiki—for soft and easy wrappings. Furoshiki can be bought in oriental import stores or you can use bandannas, large handkerchiefs, or scarves, or make your own (see Furoshiki, page 113).

The paper used in this book can be divided into four types.

1. Lightweight paper. Cellophane, crepe paper, tissue paper, some washi. Any thin, almost transparent paper.

2. Medium-weight paper. Most wrapping paper, typing paper, stationery, pages from magazines, newspapers.

3. Heavyweight paper. Thicker paper, including some wrapping paper, paper used for art posters, momi-gami (a type of washi).

4. Cardboard. Includes any heavy card stock such as that used for shoe boxes and other commercial packing. Try inserting a sheet of cardboard into a flat wrapping to protect a photograph.

For tips on selecting and sizing paper and problem solving, see More about Paper (page 32).

While neither ribbon nor mizuhiki are necessary for some of these wrapping ideas, they can and do add a nice touch to many packages. Ribbon, usually the non-woven craft type, can be bought almost everywhere that gift wrapping is sold. Look into fabric stores for woven ribbon, lace, braid, yarn, cord, or other possibilities. Rough brown package string can give a natural feeling to a gift wrapped in plain brown paper. Mizuhiki are sold in oriental import stores or you can make your own (see Mizuhiki, page 68). But do not stop at ribbon and mizuhiki. Try attaching small decorative items like pinecones, dry flowers, stickers, or flower appliques, or top the wrapping off with a card.

Gift wrapping does not require any special tools or equipment; everything you need can be found in your own home. For most of the wrappings, you will need only a pair of scissors, glue, tape, and a ruler. But check the list of materials before you begin: you may also need double-faced tape, a compass, and ordinary flexible wire or string.

A NOTE ON THE DIAGRAMS

A line of small dots indicates the inside of a fold line.

- -

A line of dots and dashes (a broken dotted line) is used to show the outside of a fold line.

— · — · — · — · — · — · — · — · —

BASIC BOXES AND CYLINDERS

*Ten imaginative and exciting ideas for
the most common shapes a gift can take.*

Boxes in the Japanese tradition
see page 13, Gifts 1–3

Boxes—the most familiar and
a slant on the most familiar
see page 20, Gifts 4–7

Cylinders—plain and fancy
see page 27, Gifts 8–10

Boxes in the Japanese tradition

One of the more traditional ways of wrapping a gift in Japan is to simply place a piece of paper over or around a box without completely covering it. This form of wrapping is not intended to conceal or protect the gift but to signify that it is indeed a present and convey the feelings of the giver. This method is particularly effective when you want to show off a pretty gift box or add a special touch to familiar shapes like boxes of chocolates or jigsaw puzzles.

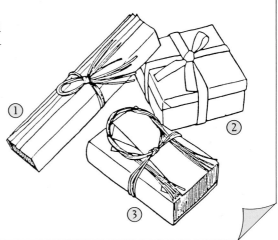

1

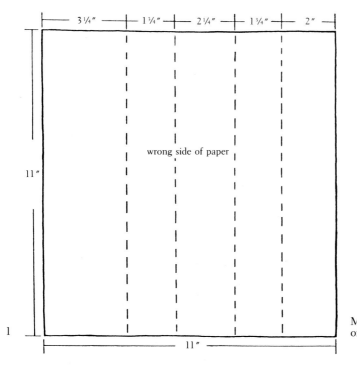

This long, narrow wooden box is wrapped in delicately shaded *washi* with colored *mizuhiki* strands tied around it. The paper has been simply wrapped around the box and folded where the edges meet to make an attractive pattern.

Materials

GIFT
Box: 1 ¾″ (height) × 2 ¼″ (width) × 11″ (length)

PAPER
11″ × 11″ medium-weight washi

OTHER MATERIALS
10 strands of 21″ mizuhiki (see page 68) in various colors

3 ¼″ · 1 ¾″ · 2 ¼″ · 1 ¾″ · 2″

wrong side of paper

11″

1

11″

Mark or score the wrong side of the paper.

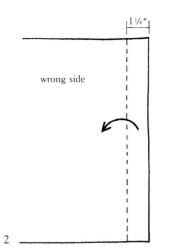

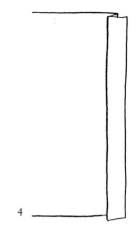

2

Fold 1 1/4″ of the right edge
to the left.

3

Fold 3/4″ of the flap to the
right.

4

The folded edge should look
like this.

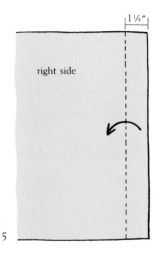

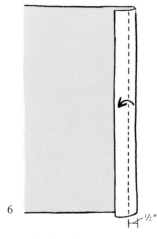

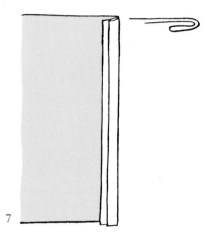

5

Turn the paper over so that
the folded edge runs along
the left side and the wrong
side faces down. Fold 1 1/4″
of the right edge to the left.

6

Fold 1/2″ of the new right
edge to the left.

7

The folded edge should look
like this.

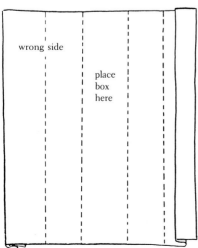

8

Turn the paper over so the wrong side is face
up, and the folds done in steps 2 and 3 run along
the right border. Place the box, bottom side
down, on the paper as shown.

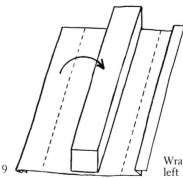

9

Wrap the box. Bring up the
left side first.

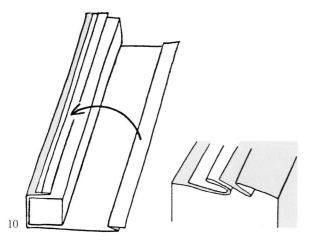

10 Bring up the right side of the paper, overlapping the left edge.

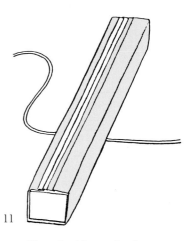

11 Place the 10 strands of *mizuhiki* under the box leaving 10″ on the left side.

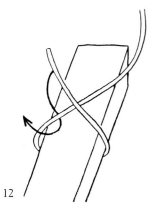

12 Cross the ends with the short end on top, then pass the short end under the long end as shown.

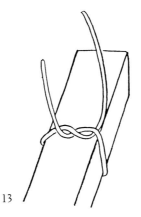

13 The knot should now look like this.

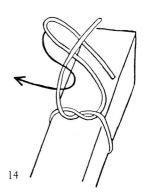

14 Cross the *mizuhiki* again with the short end over the long end. Make a loop of the long end and pass the loop over and then under the short end.

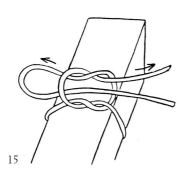

15 Gently pull the strands in the directions indicated and tighten and shape the knot.

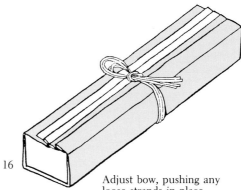

16 Adjust bow, pushing any loose strands in place.

Square wooden boxes with fitted lids were used to store utensils for the tea ceremony. The top was covered with paper, and the whole parcel tied with ribbon to keep the lid, packing, and contents in place. This wrapping can be used for a box with either a fitted lid or an ordinary lidded box.

Materials

GIFT
Box: 3″(h) × 5½″(w) × 5½″(l)

PAPER
7½″ × 7½″ *medium-weight* washi

OTHER MATERIALS
46″ of ½″ olive green ribbon

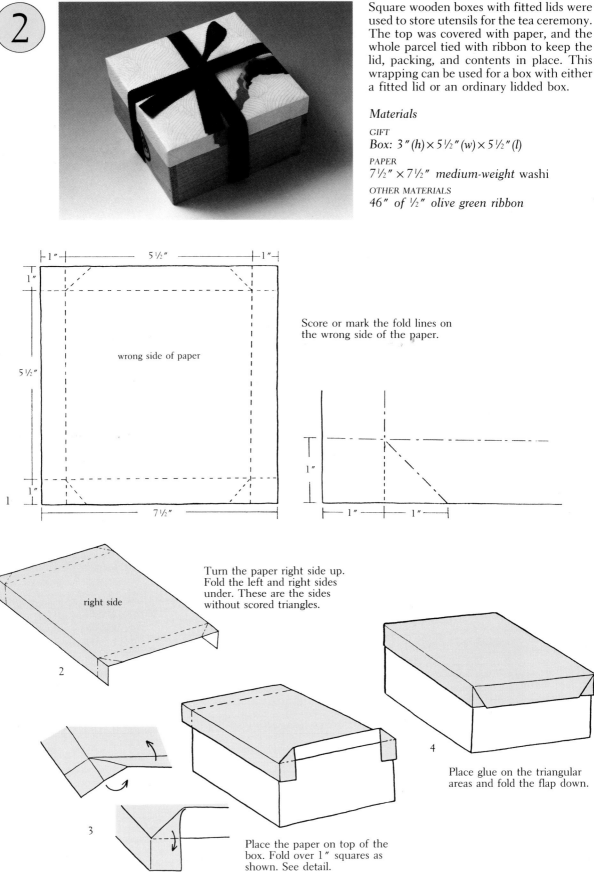

Score or mark the fold lines on the wrong side of the paper.

wrong side of paper

1″ 5½″ 1″
1″
5½″
1″
7½″

1″
1″ 1″

Turn the paper right side up. Fold the left and right sides under. These are the sides without scored triangles.

right side

2

Place glue on the triangular areas and fold the flap down.

4

3

Place the paper on top of the box. Fold over 1″ squares as shown. See detail.

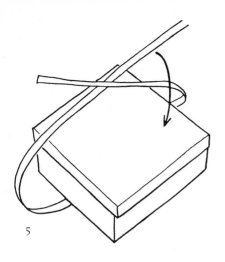

5

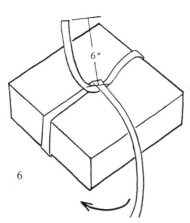

6

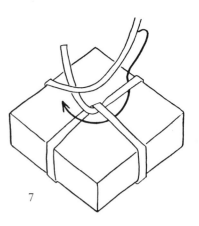

7

Place the ribbon under the box with 36″ extending to the left. Cross with the short end in front of the long end at the center of the package.

Measured from the crossing, the short end should be about 6″ and the long end 30″. Pass the long end under the box.

Cross the long end in front of the short end, then pass it under the ribbon as shown.

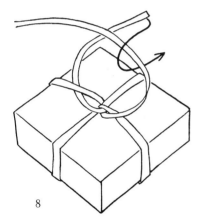

8

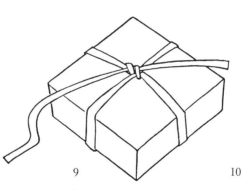

9

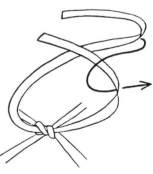

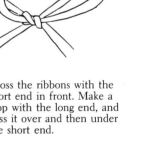

10

With the long end of the ribbon in front, take the short end and pass it over and then under the long end.

Tie.

Cross the ribbons with the short end in front. Make a loop with the long end, and pass it over and then under the short end.

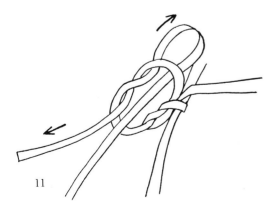

11

Gently pull the ribbon in the directions indicated by the arrows to adjust and shape.

Delicately shaded *washi* is wrapped around this rectangular box, leaving the ends open. The paper is folded where the edges meet for an understated flourish, and *mizuhiki* strands add the final touch.

Materials

GIFT
Box: 1¾″ (h) × 4″ (w) × 6½″ (l)

PAPER
6½″ × 15⅜″ *medium-weight* washi

OTHER MATERIALS·
5 *strands of 48″ gold-and-silver* mizuhiki
(see page 68)
Double-faced tape

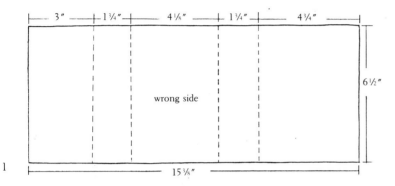

1

Score or mark fold lines on the wrong side.

2

Divide the 4¾″ section at the right into half at the top edge and measure 1½″ in from the right edge at the bottom. Fold the right edge to the left along this line.

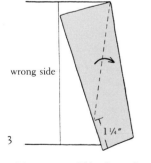

3

Measure up 1¼″ from the bottom edge, and fold the top section to the right.

4

Measure 1¼″ along the top edge, and fold back to the left.

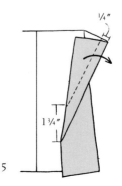

5

Measure 1¾″ along the left edge and ¼″ along the top edge as shown. Fold the flap toward the right.

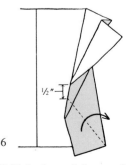

6

Fold the lower left part of the flap to the right, beginning ½″ below the starting point of the previous fold.

18 BASIC BOXES AND CYLINDERS

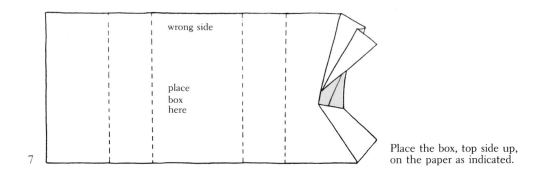

7

wrong side

place
box
here

Place the box, top side up,
on the paper as indicated.

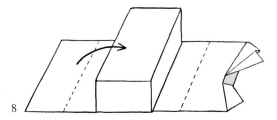
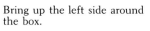
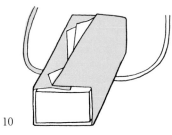

8

Bring up the left side around
the box.

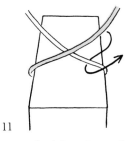

9

Bring up the right side
around the box. Secure with
double-faced tape.

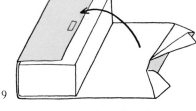

10

Center the *mizuhiki* strands
under the box with the silver
end to the left.

11

Cross the left end over the
right, then pass it under the
right end.

12

Cross the ends again (right
end in front), and pass the
left end over and then under
the other, making sure the
strands of *mizuhiki* are neatly
lined up along the edges of
the box.

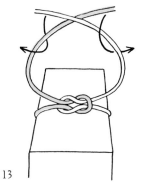

13

Tighten the knot, positioning
it in the center of the box.
Cross the ends, right end
over left.

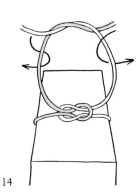

14

Wrap each end around the
other end twice.

15

Pull the ends down to make
the *mizuhiki* circle. Rest
them on the top of the box,
spreading strand ends apart
as shown in the color
photograph on page 9.

Boxes—the most familiar and a slant on the most familiar

Presented here are four elementary techniques—the familiar straight-on style (Gifts 6, 7) and the Japanese technique of wrapping at an angle (Gifts 4, 5). These dependable and versatile favorites are a splendid opportunity to experiment with unusual paper and with techniques such as layering.

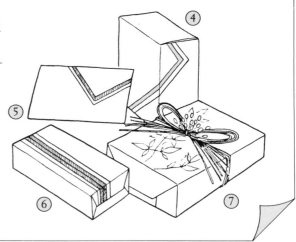

(4)
(5)
(6)
(7)

---

(4)

Wrapping at an angle is probably the most common method in Japan. It produces an arresting asymmetric wrap that is attractive from any side. Layering accentuates the diagonal line of the final flap of paper.

Materials

GIFT
Box: 2¾″ (h) × 5½″ (w) × 5½″ (l)

PAPER
13¾″ × 17¾″ *medium-weight* washi, *1 sheet each of yellow, aqua, and brown*

To determine the proper size of paper for your box, see the instructions on page 32. For best results when layering, shorten the length of the paper produced by the formula by 10 percent.

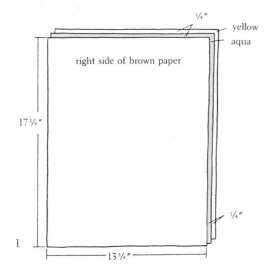

¼″
yellow
aqua
right side of brown paper
17¾″
¼″
1
13¾″

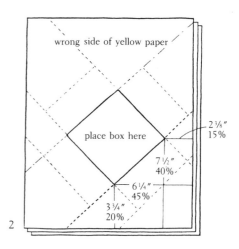

wrong side of yellow paper
2⅛″ 15%
place box here
7½″ 40%
6¼″ 45%
3¾″ 20%
2

Layer the three sheets of *washi* so that a ¼″ band of aqua and of yellow are showing along the top and right edges. Glue the three sheets together lightly to prevent shifting. Try to glue a spot that will not be noticeable.

With the wrong side of the yellow paper face up, position the box as shown. (If not layering, place the box upside down on the paper.) Use the percentages given to determine approximate position of the box. Once familiar with the technique, you will easily be able to position the box correctly. The three overlapping sheets should be visible along the right and bottom edges.

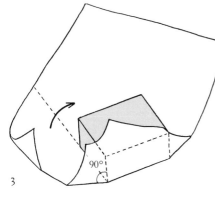

3

Fold up the lower right-hand corner of the paper.

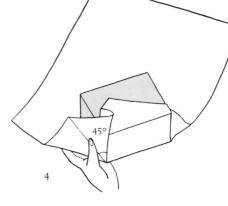

4

Bring up the paper to the left of the box and align the outer fold line with the vertical edge of the box, using your thumb to guide the excess paper inward to produce 45° folds. Do not push all the excess paper inward, but only enough to align the paper to the edge of the box. A flap of excess paper should be peeking out at the top of the box.

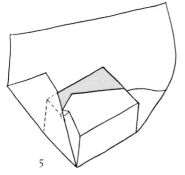

5

Note that this flap is at right angles to the top of the box.

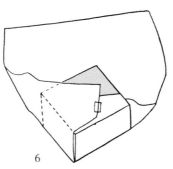

6

Fold the paper over the box (covering flap) and tape down.

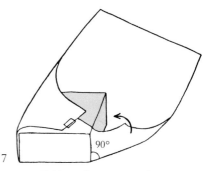

7

Fold up the paper to the right of the box.

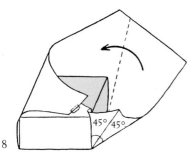

8

Again, guiding the excess paper inward with your thumb, align the folded edge with the vertical edge of the box. This time there will be only a small flap peeking up over the edge.

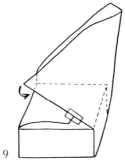

9

Fold the paper over the box and tape down. Fold the flap of paper sticking out beyond the left edge under along the edge of the box.

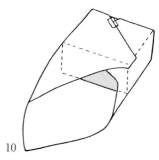

10

Turn the box around.

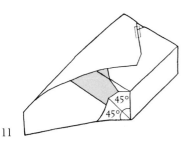

11

Bring up the paper on the right side of the package, guiding the paper inward with your index finger and aligning the folded edge with the box. While pushing paper inward, crease it. Unfold.

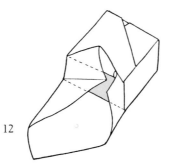

12

Repeat step 11 with the left side. Unfold.

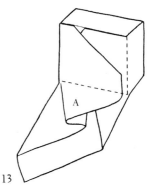

13

Roll the box toward you onto its side. Make sure the paper along crease A does not get folded under the box. Crease A should be sharp and run along the edge of the box.

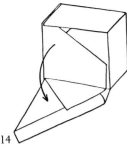

14

Roll the box over once more so the bottom faces up.

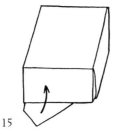

15

Fold up the small layered flap. Glue. (If you are not using layering, simply tuck the flap under so it is not visible and use the side facing you as the top of the box.)

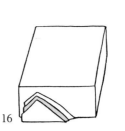

16

Flip the box over so the decorative layering faces up.

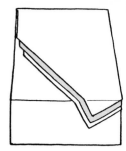

5

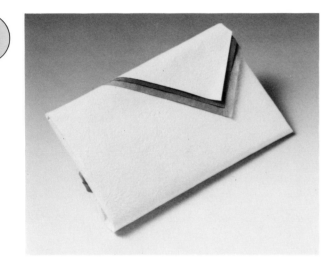

When the box or gift is rectangular but there is not enough height to make attractive corners, you can still wrap the gift at an angle. Perfect for address books, small notebooks, candy bars, or thin boxes.

Materials

GIFT
Box (or gift itself): ⅛″(h) × 4¼″(w) × 7″(l)
PAPER
*10½″ × 16″ medium-weight washi,
1 sheet each of white, pink, and yellow*

To determine the proper size of paper for your gift, see the instructions on page 32. For best results when layering, increase the formula length of this wrapping by 10 percent and decrease the width by 5 percent.

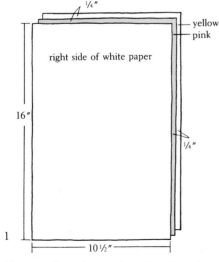

Place the three sheets of *washi* on top of each other, right sides up. One-fourth inch of the edges of the yellow and red sheets should show on the right and top edges. Glue the three sheets together in an inconspicuous spot.

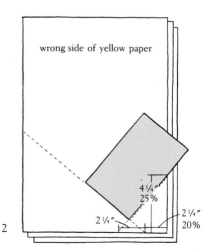

With the wrong side of the yellow paper face up and the layered edges at bottom right, place the box on the paper as indicated. Use the percentages given to determine the approximate position of the box. (After a few times, the position is easy to judge.) Note that one corner of the gift sticks out beyond the paper.

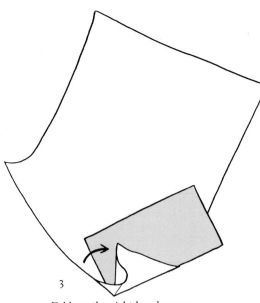

3

Fold up the right-hand corner
of the paper, then fold in the
paper to the left of the
package, aligning the lower
fold with the lower edge of
the gift.

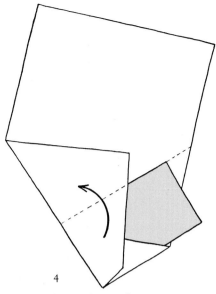

4

Roll the gift away from you,
folding along the dotted line.
Make sure the edges along
the left are aligned.

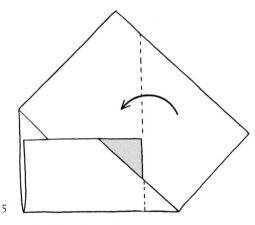

5

Position the package as
shown. Fold up the paper to
the right, aligning the bottom
fold with the bottom edge of
the gift.

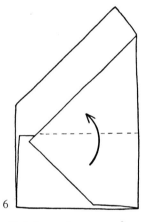

6

Roll the package away from
you once more, folding along
the dotted line. Align the
paper along the left and right
edges of the gift.

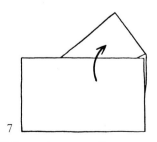

7

Roll the package away from you a third
time. Glue the flap. (If you are not using
layering, simply tuck the last flap under so
it is hidden. If shorter paper is used, this
step may not be necessary at all.)

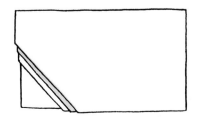

6

Effective use of layering and decorative folds transforms a simple wrapping into something special. For variation, try moving the folded edges to the center or to the other side.

Materials

GIFT
Box: 1¾″(h) × 3½″(w) × 6¼″(l)
PAPER
9¼″ × 15½″ washi, 1 sheet each of medium-weight beige and lightweight pink

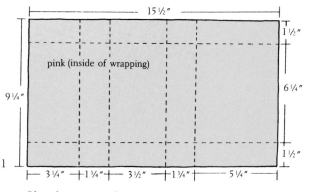

1 Glue the wrong sides together. Use the beige side as the outside. On the pink side (now the wrong side), score or mark the fold lines to indicate where the box goes.

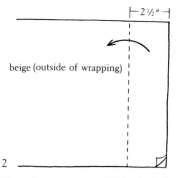

2 Turn the paper over. With the beige side facing up, fold 2½″ of the right edge to the left.

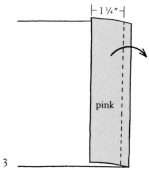

3 Fold 1¾″ of the flap back to the right.

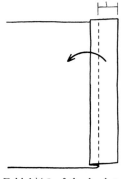

4 Fold 1¼″ of the back to the left.

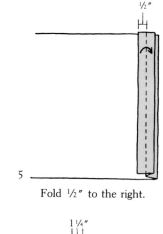

5 Fold ½″ to the right.

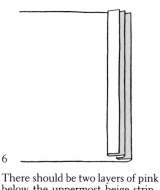

6 There should be two layers of pink below the uppermost beige strip.

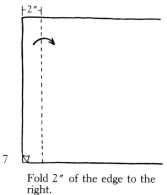

7 Fold 2″ of the edge to the right.

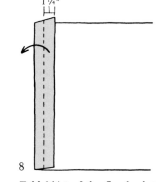

8 Fold 1¼″ of the flap back to the left.

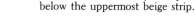

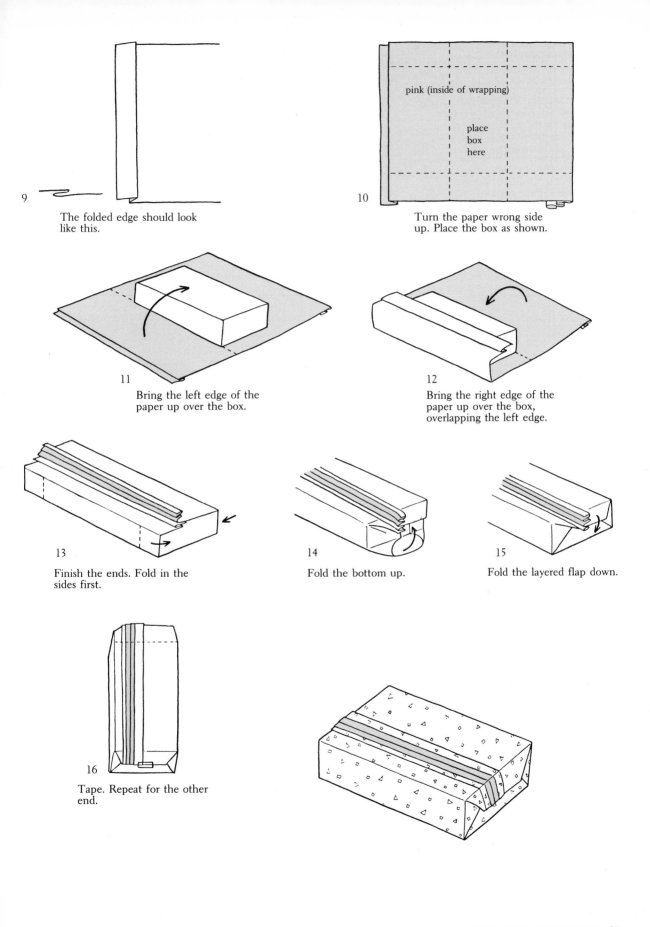

9   The folded edge should look like this.

10   Turn the paper wrong side up. Place the box as shown.

pink (inside of wrapping)

place
box
here

11   Bring the left edge of the paper up over the box.

12   Bring the right edge of the paper up over the box, overlapping the left edge.

13   Finish the ends. Fold in the sides first.

14   Fold the bottom up.

15   Fold the layered flap down.

16   Tape. Repeat for the other end.

7

Dried leaves and small red berries enliven this familiar method of wrapping. Inserting a photograph, magazine clipping, or a sticker will add a personal or playful touch.

Materials

GIFT
Box: 3″(h)×5¾″(w)×7″(l)

PAPER
2 sheets of 12″×19″ lightweight washi with dried leaves inserted between them

Any sort of transparent paper may be used for the outside layer, and medium-weight paper may be used for the lower layer. To determine the proper size of paper for your box, see the instructions on page 32.

OTHER MATERIALS
7 strands of 40″ colored mizuhiki (see page 68)
Artificial red berries

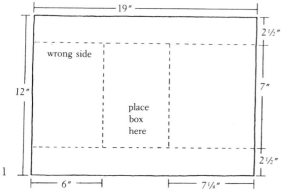

Mark or score the position of the top of the box on the paper. Insert the leaves and arrange in an attractive pattern. Glue lightly.

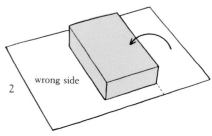

Place the box upside down in the position indicated.

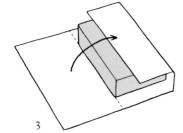

Fold up the paper to the left side of the box.

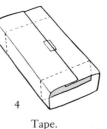

Tape.

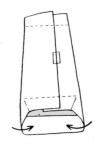

Finish the ends next. Fold in both sides of the paper, then fold down the top flap.

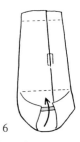

Fold up the bottom flap.

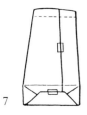

Tape. Finish the other end in the same way.

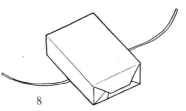

Turn the box over. Center the *mizuhiki* strands underneath the box.

Tie in a bow. Add berries.

Cylinders—plain and fancy

These three basic methods can be used to wrap cylinders of all shapes and sizes— from candles and pencil holders to ashtrays and vases. The Japanese technique of using the paper at an angle also works for cylinders.

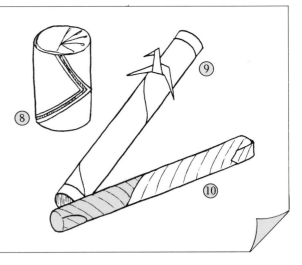

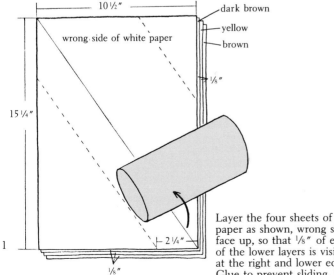

Wrapping on an angle produces an interesting triangular flap—a perfect place to use layering—and attractive folds on the top and bottom.

Materials

GIFT
Cylinder: 5½″(h) × 2¾″(diameter)

PAPER
10½″ × 15¼″ lightweight washi, 1 sheet each of white, dark brown, yellow, and brown

When measured diagonally, the paper should be about 1½ times the circumference of the cylinder and at the same time more than the sum of 2 times the diameter and 2 times the height of the cylinder.

10½″

dark brown

yellow

brown

wrong side of white paper

⅛″

15¼″

1

2¼″

⅛″

Layer the four sheets of paper as shown, wrong sides face up, so that ⅛″ of each of the lower layers is visible at the right and lower edges. Glue to prevent sliding. Place the cylinder as shown with its edge approximately 2¼″ from the right edge of the paper.

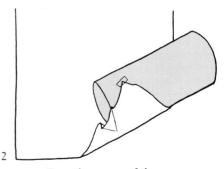

2

Tape the corner of the paper onto the cylinder.

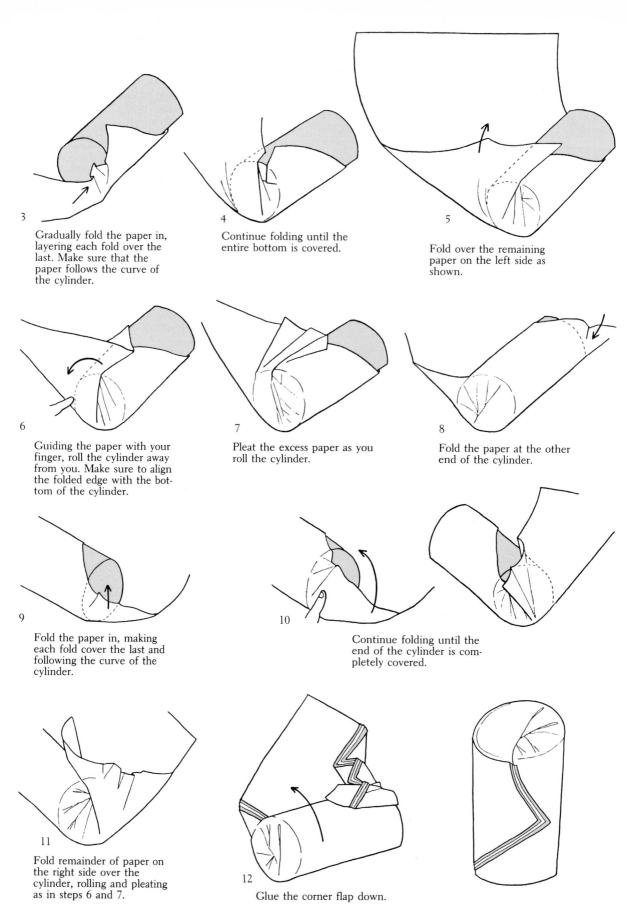

3 Gradually fold the paper in, layering each fold over the last. Make sure that the paper follows the curve of the cylinder.

4 Continue folding until the entire bottom is covered.

5 Fold over the remaining paper on the left side as shown.

6 Guiding the paper with your finger, roll the cylinder away from you. Make sure to align the folded edge with the bottom of the cylinder.

7 Pleat the excess paper as you roll the cylinder.

8 Fold the paper at the other end of the cylinder.

9 Fold the paper in, making each fold cover the last and following the curve of the cylinder.

10 Continue folding until the end of the cylinder is completely covered.

11 Fold remainder of paper on the right side over the cylinder, rolling and pleating as in steps 6 and 7.

12 Glue the corner flap down.

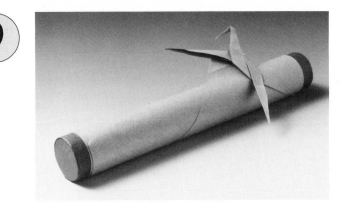

This gift is wrapped first with an underlayer of gray paper and then covered again by green paper with a crane folded into it. This outer sheet originally was made from *washi* and placed like a napkin or paper doily under Japanese sweets served on a plate.

Materials

GIFT
Cylinder: 1¾″(d) × 12″(l)

PAPER
6¼″ × 13¼″ medium-weight gray paper
10½″ × 16½″ light green, medium-weight paper (for crane)
1¾″ (d) medium-weight red circles of paper, 2 sheets (for ends of cylinder)

To determine the paper size of the outer layer, subtract 1″ or 2″ from the length of the cylinder and make this the width of the paper. For length, add the circumference of the cylinder to the width of the paper.

OTHER MATERIALS
Compass
Double-faced tape

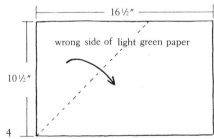

1

gray paper

6¼″

13¼″

1¾″

1¾″

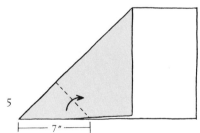

2

wrong side

Place the cylinder on the wrong side of the gray paper with equal amounts of paper at each end. Roll up the paper and the cylinder, and tape.

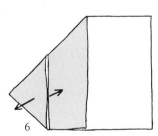

3

Fold in the paper at the ends, pleating the paper as you go. Cover the ends with the round red circles of paper, securing with double-faced tape or glue.

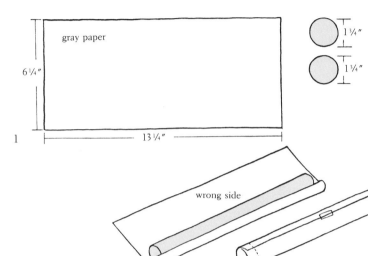

4

16½″

10½″

wrong side of light green paper

With the wrong side of the light green paper face up, fold down the upper left corner so the left edge is aligned with the bottom edge.

5

7″

Measure 7″ from the corner and fold up, making sure the upper edges are aligned.

6

Open the 7″ triangle as shown.

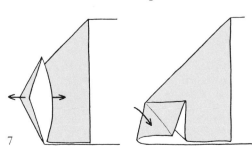

7

Flatten the opened triangle into a square, aligning the fold line splitting the square with the folded edge underneath.

8

Fold the corners of the square in and align at the center.

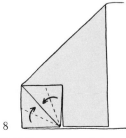

9

Crease the folds made in the previous step. Unfold.

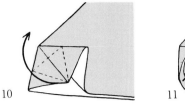

10

Lift the lower right corner and open the square, folding back along the dotted line.

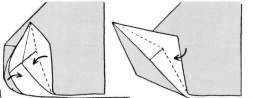
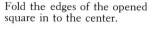

11

Fold the edges of the opened square in to the center.

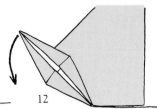

12

Turn the paper as shown.

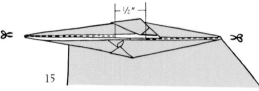

13

Fold in the upper left and lower right edges of the diamond, aligning at the center.

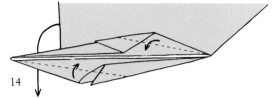

14

Fold in the remaining edges of the diamond, aligning at the center. Pick up the paper and bring the large unfolded area toward you, so that the folded diamond is at the top.

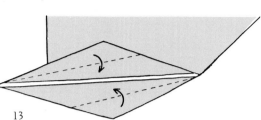

15

Cut open the center of the diamond, leaving ½″ in the middle section uncut.

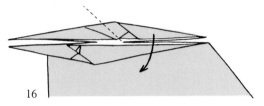

16

Fold the upper right section down along the dotted line.

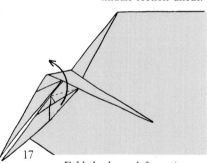

17

Fold the lower left section up along the dotted line.

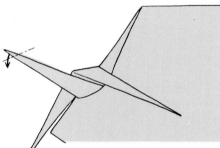

18

Fold the point of the folded section back along the dotted line.

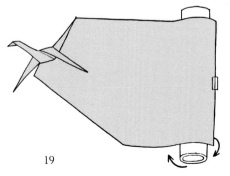

19

Tape the end of the green paper opposite the crane onto the cylinder and wrap the paper around the cylinder.

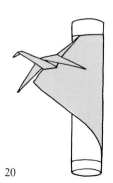

20

Use glue on the back of the crane to secure the crane and wrapping.

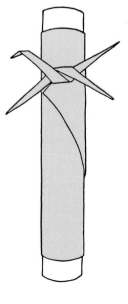

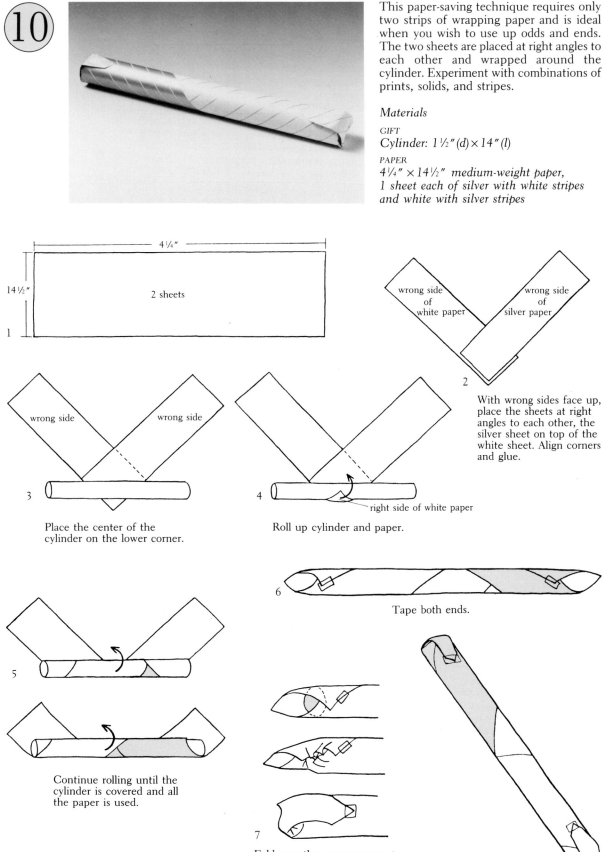

This paper-saving technique requires only two strips of wrapping paper and is ideal when you wish to use up odds and ends. The two sheets are placed at right angles to each other and wrapped around the cylinder. Experiment with combinations of prints, solids, and stripes.

Materials

GIFT
Cylinder: 1½″(d) × 14″(l)

PAPER
4¼″ × 14½″ medium-weight paper, 1 sheet each of silver with white stripes and white with silver stripes

4¼″

14½″

2 sheets

1

wrong side of white paper

wrong side of silver paper

2

With wrong sides face up, place the sheets at right angles to each other, the silver sheet on top of the white sheet. Align corners and glue.

3 wrong side   wrong side

Place the center of the cylinder on the lower corner.

4

right side of white paper

Roll up cylinder and paper.

5

Continue rolling until the cylinder is covered and all the paper is used.

6

Tape both ends.

7

Fold over the excess paper at the top and bottom, and tape.

More about Paper

WHEN SELECTING PAPER

The size, shape, and characteristics of the gift, the age and personality of the recipient, and season and occasion should all be taken into consideration when selecting paper. While almost any kind of paper is attractive when wrapping a medium-sized package, solid colors or large prints and stripes in orthodox, subtle color combinations are more likely to be effective when wrapping large gifts. Small gifts will look their best when wrapped in solid colors or small prints. Use color as an accent, making effective use of layering or ribbons.

Soft paper reveals the shape of the gift and can add a warm, gentle touch to a gift. Use soft paper for wrappings in which paper is gathered instead of folded (see Gifts 18, 27, 45). Medium-weight paper can be used for most wrappings and is the best paper to use when it is necessary to produce intricate folds. Stiff paper can be made into various shapes and produces a wrapping with simple, well-defined lines (see Gifts 13, 14). Decorative folds made with stiff paper will hold their shape well.

It is not necessary to limit yourself to one sheet of wrapping paper. You can create appealing packages by layering paper (see Gifts 30, 31, 33, 40, 42, 43) or sliding the top layer to reveal part of the bottom sheet (see Gifts 4, 5, 6, 8, 14, 20, 39). Nor is it necessary to always use wrapping paper. Try such materials as waxed paper, cellophane, vinyl, cardboard, cloth, or paper doilies (see Gifts 26, 45, 46, 47, 51, 55).

HOW TO DETERMINE THE SIZE OF PAPER NEEDED

The methods described below are standard formulas. Variations may be necessary when the box to be wrapped is extremely large or small or when a special effect is desired.

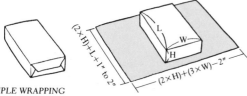

SIMPLE WRAPPING

To determine how much paper is needed to wrap a square or rectangular box, use the following two formulas.

Width = (2 × box height) + length + 1″ to 2″
Length = (2 × box height) + (3 × box width) − 2″

This simple wrapping method is particularly effective when the box to be wrapped is very large. When wrapping a box containing a cake or something that cannot be flipped over, wrap the paper around the top of the box and overlap it underneath.

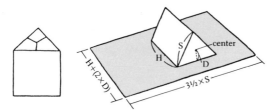

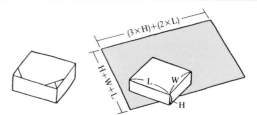

WRAPPING ON THE SLANT

In Japan, this method of wrapping square or rectangular boxes is used perhaps even more often than the simple wrapping described in the previous section. These formulas are very basic. To make sure that you have enough paper, measure the paper diagonally from corner to corner. It should be at least twice the sum of the length, width, and height of the box. Use the formulas below to determine what size paper is necessary.

Width = box height + box width + box length
Length = (3 × box height) + (2 × box length)

Wrapping on a slant produces a package with all the folds meeting evenly at the corners. Thus when viewed from the side there are no ugly folds (see Gifts 4, 5, 54).

WRAPPING TRIANGULAR BOXES

Use these formulas and the paper will meet in the center of the triangular surface at the ends of the box.

Width = box height + (2 × distance from triangle center to side)
Length = 3½ × side of triangle

WHEN YOU HAVE TROUBLE

WHEN THE GIFT IS TOO BIG FOR ONE SHEET OF PAPER

- *Use double-faced tape, making sure the tape is not visible from the outside, and join two pieces of paper.*
- *Combine two sheets of compatible paper and make the difference part of the design (see 10, 49)*
- *Forget about covering the whole gift and wrap part of it (see Gifts 1, 2, 3, 19, 21).*

WHEN THE PAPER TEARS

- *Cover the spot with a sticker.*
- *Cut the hole into an interesting shape—a square or circle, a star, a tree, a bell—and make it work for you (see Gifts 15, 52).*

USING THE SHAPE OF THE OBJECT

*Wrap towels, scarves, candies and cakes,
bottles and jars, and even flowers and
plants as they are—without a box.*

Soft additions
see page 41, Gifts 11–12

Softness itself
see page 45, Gifts 13–17

Bottles and jars
see page 50, Gifts 18–22

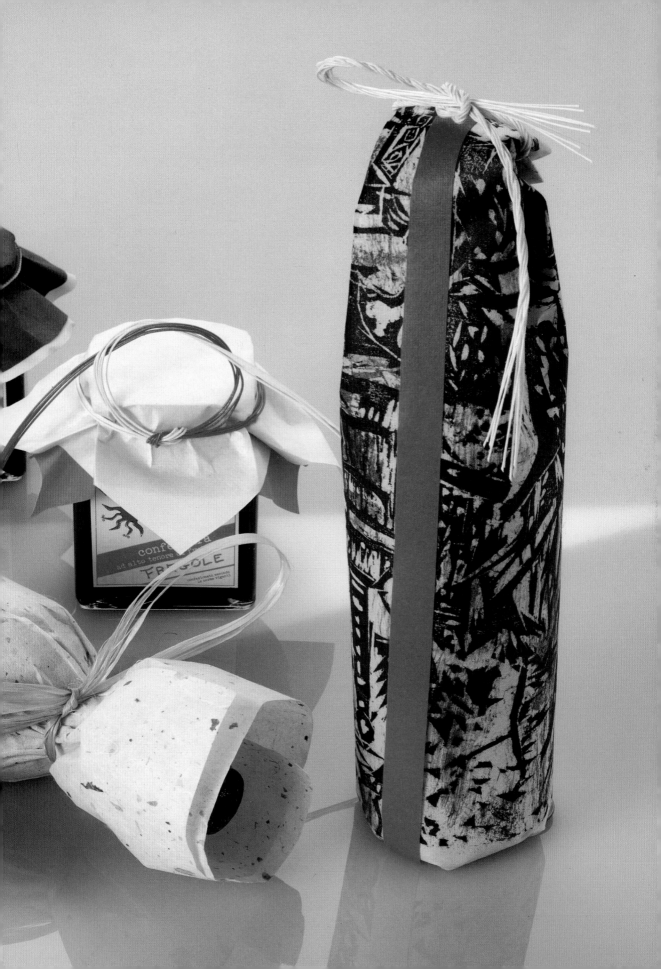

The best things come
in small packages
see page 57, Gifts 23–29

Flowers and plants
see page 65, Gifts 30–31

Soft additions

The crane and the noshi, *both traditional Japanese shapes, can be placed on any package with rounded corners. Experiment with different combinations of colors and textures.*

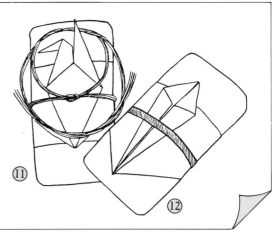

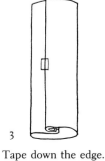

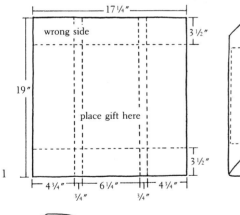

This crane, also shown on the jacket of this book, is adapted from a traditional Japanese envelope used to give money on auspicious occasions.

Materials

GIFT
Towel (dimensions when folded):
$\frac{3}{4}"$ (h) × $6\frac{1}{4}"$ (w) × $12"$ (l)

PAPER
$17\frac{1}{4}"$ × $19"$ *medium-weight paper, red with white polka dots (for simple wrapping)*
$14\frac{1}{4}"$ × $20\frac{3}{4}"$ *medium-weight paper, white decorated with small bunches of flowers (for crane)*

OTHER MATERIALS
5 strands of 6 ft. silver-and-gold mizuhiki *(see page 68)*

SIMPLE WRAPPING

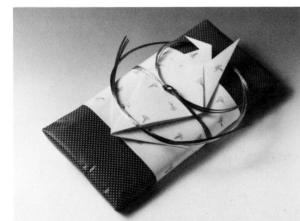

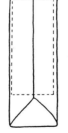

Place the towel in the center of the red paper as shown. Fold up the left and right sides of the paper and bring the edges together.

2

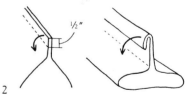

Fold $\frac{1}{2}"$ of the edges down. Keeping the edges together, fold the paper at the center of the gift to the left.

3

Tape down the edge.

4

Next, finish the end. Fold in the sides.

5

Position the top flap directly over the bottom flap.

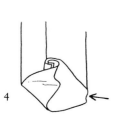

6

Fold both flaps up and tape.

7

Finish the other end in the same manner.

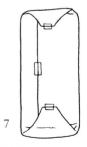

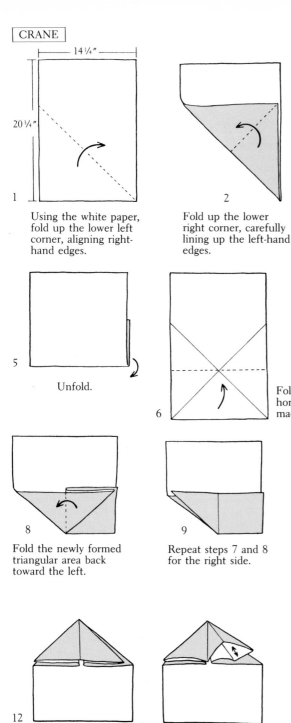

14 1/4"

20 3/4"

1 — Using the white paper, fold up the lower left corner, aligning right-hand edges.

2 — Fold up the lower right corner, carefully lining up the left-hand edges.

3 — Unfold.

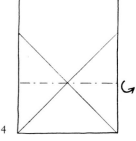

4 — Fold the bottom half under along the dotted line.

5 — Unfold.

6 — Fold up along the horizontal crease made in step 4.

7 — Holding the center lightly in place with your thumb, fold the left side of the flap over as shown.

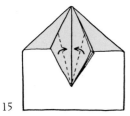

8 — Fold the newly formed triangular area back toward the left.

9 — Repeat steps 7 and 8 for the right side.

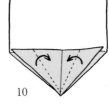

10 — Fold the upper left and right triangular sections over as shown. They should meet at the center.

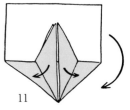

11 — Open folds made in the previous step, and rotate the paper 180°.

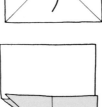

12 — Open the right-hand triangle. Flatten and center to form a diamond.

13 — Fold the left half of the diamond to the right.

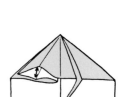

14 — Repeat step 12 with the left-hand triangle.

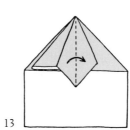

15 — Fold the sides of the diamond made from the left-hand triangle in to meet at the center as shown. (Be sure to use only the uppermost right layer.)

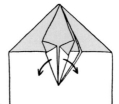

16 — Open the folds made in step 15.

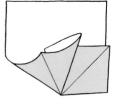
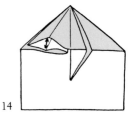
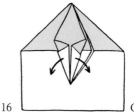

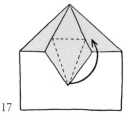

17 Bring the lower point of the diamond up to meet the top of the diamond, folding in the upper layer of the sides and aligning at the center.

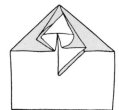

18 Fold the point of the diamond down.

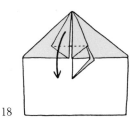

19 Fold the right half of the diamond and the layer of paper below it to the left to form a new diamond.

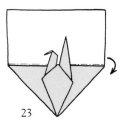

20

Repeat steps 15 to 18. Fold the upper left side of the diamond to the right. Rotate the wrapping 180°.

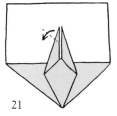

21 Crease along the dotted line.

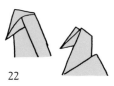

22 Fold the paper in as shown to form the beak of the crane.

23 Fold the unused top part of the paper under.

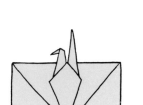

24 Center the crane on the wrapped gift and tuck the left and right edges under.

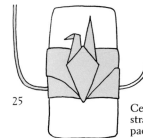

25 Center the *mizuhiki* strands under the package with the silver end to the left.

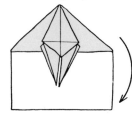

26 Cross the silver end over the gold. Pass the silver end under the gold end.

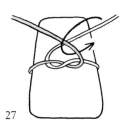

27 Cross the silver end over the gold again, and pass the gold end over and then under the silver.

28 Cross the gold end over the silver, and pass the silver end over and then under the gold end.

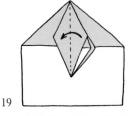

29 Tighten the top loop slightly.

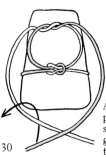

30 At the bottom of the package, cross the silver end over the gold end and bring the silver end under and then over it.

31

Tighten the loop and wrap the ends around each other to form a large circle.

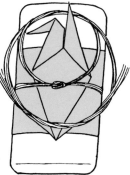

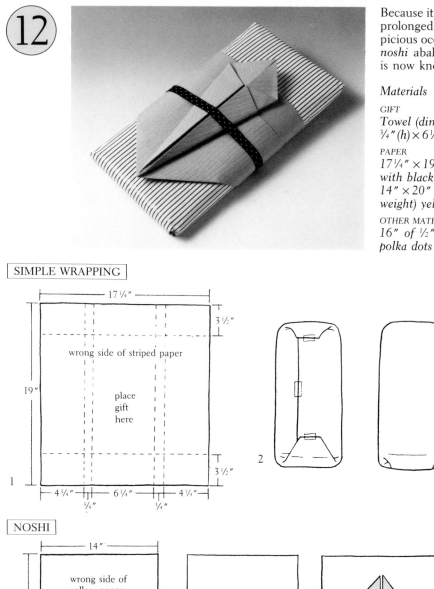

Because it was believed that eating abalone prolonged life, abalone was given on auspicious occasions in Japan. This was called *noshi* abalone. The diamond shape itself is now known as *noshi*.

Materials

GIFT
Towel (dimensions when folded):
¾″ (h) × 6¼″ (w) × 12″ (l)
PAPER
17¼″ × 19″ medium-weight paper, white with black stripes (for simple wrapping)
14″ × 20″ heavyweight (or medium-weight) yellow paper (for noshi)

OTHER MATERIALS
16″ of ½″ cloth ribbon, black with white polka dots

SIMPLE WRAPPING

17¼″

3½″

wrong side of striped paper

19″

place
gift
here

3½″

1

4¾″   6¼″   4¾″
   ¾″   ¾″

2

Wrap gift with striped paper following the "simple wrapping" procedure (see Gift 11, steps 1 to 7).

NOSHI

14″

wrong side of yellow paper

20″

1

2 Follow steps 1 through 10 for the crane in Gift 11.

3 Fold in the edges again as shown.

4″

4 Fold the top 4″ of the paper under.

5 Center the *noshi* on the wrapped gift and tuck the left and right edges under.

6 Wrap the ribbon around the package and tape it in back.

Softness itself

These soft, boxless wrappings have no hard fold lines and thus preserve the softness of the presents themselves.

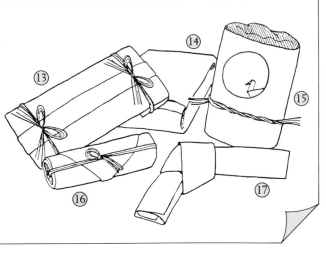

This style of wrapping is an adaptation of the package used to wrap silk kimono. Even today, kimono are folded flat and stored in *washi* which protects them from Japan's humid climate.

Materials

GIFT
Scarf or handkerchief (dimensions when folded): $\frac{1}{4}''(h) \times 6''(w) \times 10''(l)$

PAPER
Heavyweight momi-gami (a type of washi), *pink on the right side and white on the wrong side, 1 sheet of* $16'' \times 17\frac{1}{2}''$, *4 sheets of* $1\frac{3}{4}'' \times 1\frac{3}{4}''$

OTHER MATERIALS
16 strands of 12'' white mizuhiki *(see page 68)*

Divide the *mizuhiki* strands into four groups of four strands each. Place four loose *mizuhiki* ends on each small $1\frac{3}{4}''$ square and glue in place as shown. With the right side of the paper face up, fold $1\frac{1}{2}''$ of the left edge toward the right.

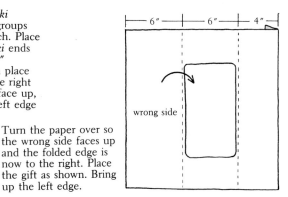

Turn the paper over so the wrong side faces up and the folded edge is now to the right. Place the gift as shown. Bring up the left edge.

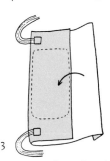

3 Bring up the right edge.

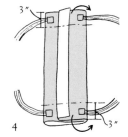

4 Fold 3″ of the top and bottom under.

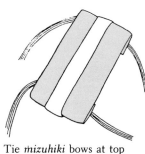

5 Tie *mizuhiki* bows at top and bottom.

14

This easy gift wrapping needs no tape, glue, or ribbon—only the paper itself.

Materials

GIFT
Scarf (dimensions when folded):
2″(h)×9″(w)×6½″(l)

PAPER
15½″×30″ heavyweight momi-gami *(a type of* washi), *1 sheet each of white and purple*

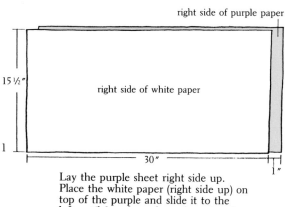

right side of purple paper

15½″

right side of white paper

1

30″

1″

Lay the purple sheet right side up. Place the white paper (right side up) on top of the purple and slide it to the left until 1″ of purple peeks out at the right.

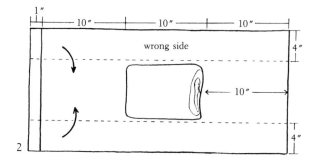

1″

10″   10″   10″

wrong side

4″

10″

4″

2

Turn the sheets over so that a 1″ band of white appears on the left-hand side. Place gift as shown. Fold 4″ of the top and bottom edges over the gift.

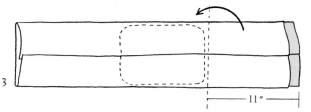

3

11″

Fold in 11″ from the right side. Do not crease too sharply.

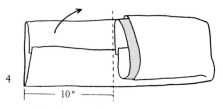

4

10″

Fold in 10″ from the left. Do not crease too sharply.

5

Insert the left edges in the pouch formed by the right layered edges.

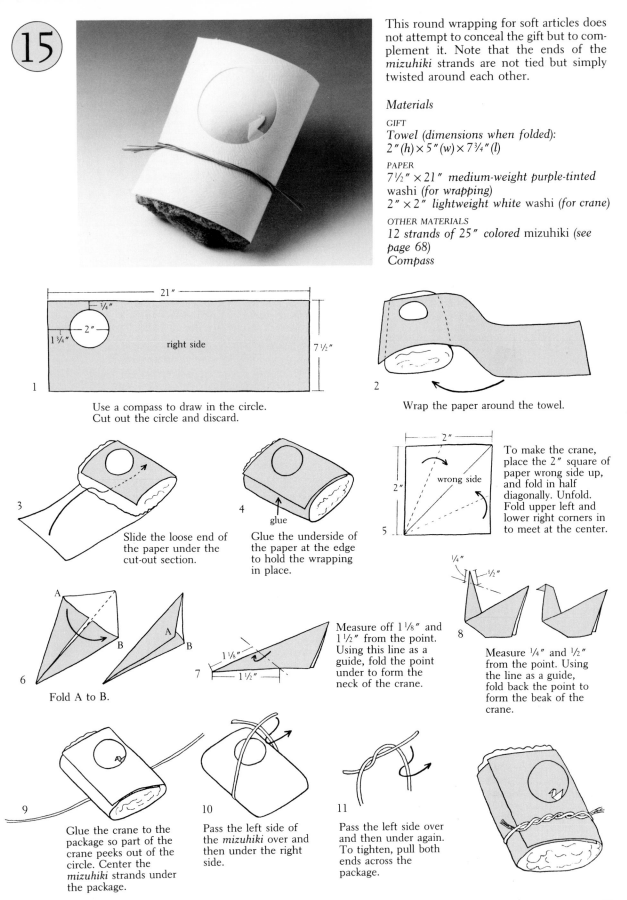

15

This round wrapping for soft articles does not attempt to conceal the gift but to complement it. Note that the ends of the *mizuhiki* strands are not tied but simply twisted around each other.

Materials

GIFT
Towel (dimensions when folded):
2″(h) × 5″(w) × 7¾″(l)

PAPER
7½″ × 21″ *medium-weight purple-tinted* washi *(for wrapping)*
2″ × 2″ *lightweight white* washi *(for crane)*

OTHER MATERIALS
12 strands of 25″ colored mizuhiki *(see page 68)*
Compass

1. — 21″ — ¾″ — 2″ — 1¾″ — right side — 7½″
Use a compass to draw in the circle. Cut out the circle and discard.

2. Wrap the paper around the towel.

3. Slide the loose end of the paper under the cut-out section.

4. glue
Glue the underside of the paper at the edge to hold the wrapping in place.

5. — 2″ — 2″ — wrong side
To make the crane, place the 2″ square of paper wrong side up, and fold in half diagonally. Unfold. Fold upper left and lower right corners in to meet at the center.

6. A B A B
Fold A to B.

7. 1⅛″ 1½″
Measure off 1⅛″ and 1½″ from the point. Using this line as a guide, fold the point under to form the neck of the crane.

8. ¼″ ½″
Measure ¼″ and ½″ from the point. Using the line as a guide, fold back the point to form the beak of the crane.

9. Glue the crane to the package so part of the crane peeks out of the circle. Center the *mizuhiki* strands under the package.

10. Pass the left side of the *mizuhiki* over and then under the right side.

11. Pass the left side over and then under again. To tighten, pull both ends across the package.

16

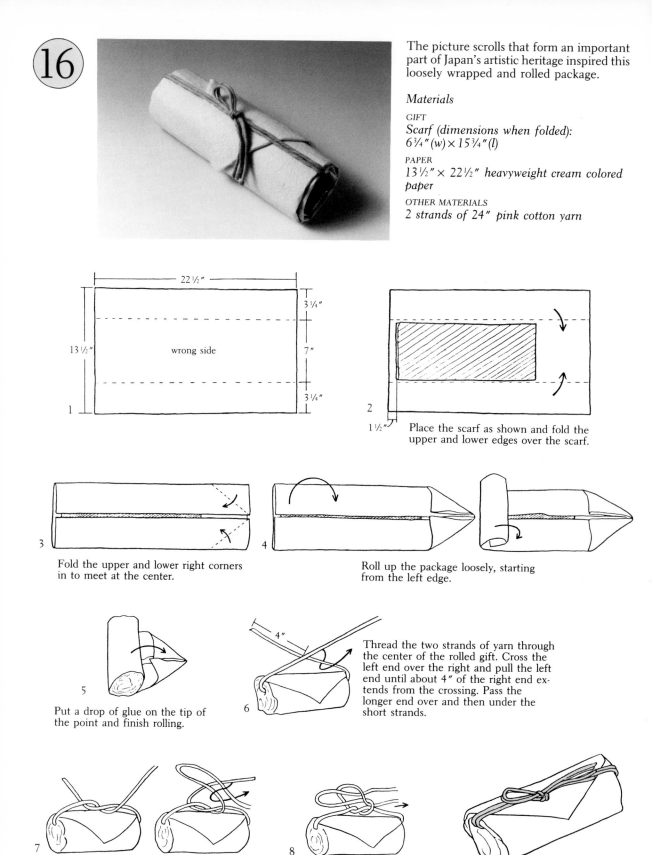

The picture scrolls that form an important part of Japan's artistic heritage inspired this loosely wrapped and rolled package.

Materials

GIFT
Scarf (dimensions when folded):
6¾″(w) × 15¾″(l)

PAPER
13½″ × 22½″ heavyweight cream colored paper

OTHER MATERIALS
2 strands of 24″ pink cotton yarn

2 Place the scarf as shown and fold the upper and lower edges over the scarf.

3 Fold the upper and lower right corners in to meet at the center.

4 Roll up the package loosely, starting from the left edge.

5 Put a drop of glue on the tip of the point and finish rolling.

6 Thread the two strands of yarn through the center of the rolled gift. Cross the left end over the right and pull the left end until about 4″ of the right end extends from the crossing. Pass the longer end over and then under the short strands.

7 Make a loop of the long end. Cross the loop over the short end, and pass the short end over and then under the loop.

8 Pull the loop and the short end to tighten and shape the knot.

17

It is said that hundreds of years ago in Japan, people simply folded and tied a love letter into a knot, and at a discreet moment slipped it into the sleeves of their lover's kimono. The simple wrapping presented here duplicates the shape of those ancient love letters.

Materials

GIFT
Scarf (dimensions when folded in fourths lengthwise): 1 ¼" (w) × 20" (l)

PAPER
8 ¼" × 23" medium-weight green, white, and yellow gradated paper

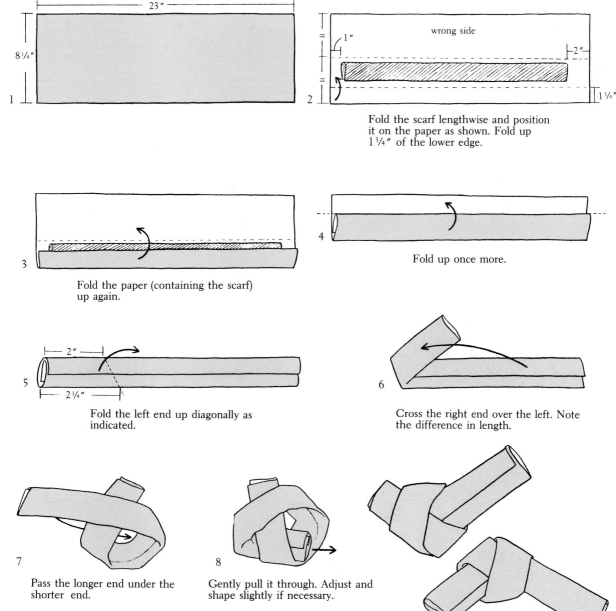

1.

2. Fold the scarf lengthwise and position it on the paper as shown. Fold up 1 ¾" of the lower edge.

3. Fold the paper (containing the scarf) up again.

4. Fold up once more.

5. Fold the left end up diagonally as indicated.

6. Cross the right end over the left. Note the difference in length.

7. Pass the longer end under the shorter end.

8. Gently pull it through. Adjust and shape slightly if necessary.

Bottles and jars

Wrapping a bottle or a jar presents problems just not found when dealing with a box. These attractive ideas will make wrapping bottles of wine and jars of homemade jam much easier.

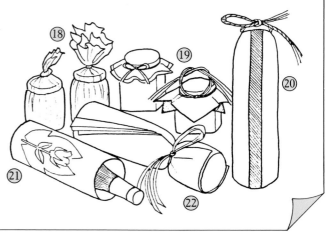

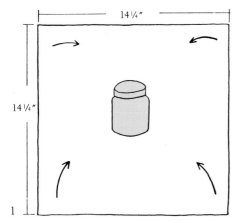

These simple two-colored wrappings present many possibilities for variation. Try cutting and shaping the top into a flower or twisting it into fanciful shapes.

Materials

GIFT
Jar of jam: 3¾" (h) × 2¼" (lid diameter), 2 jars

PAPER
14¼" × 14¼" lightweight washi
Jar A: 1 sheet of white, 2 sheets of orange
Jar B: 1 sheet of yellow-green, 1 sheet of green

OTHER MATERIALS
String or thin wire

1. Use the orange paper for Jar A and the yellow-green paper for Jar B. Place the jam in the center of the paper and bring up the corners.

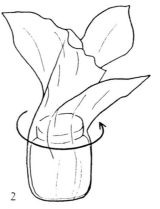

2. Use wire or string to close the wrapping around the jar.

3. Cut off the excess paper slightly above the wire or string.

4. Open up the cut-off area and flatten it, hiding the wire.

5. Spread the cut-off area out completely.

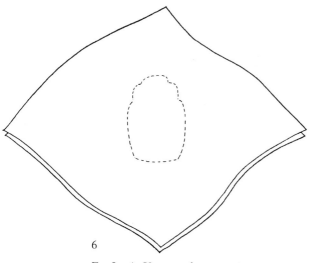

6

For Jar A: Use one sheet
each of orange and white.
For Jar B: Use the green
paper. Cover the top of the
jar with the paper as shown.

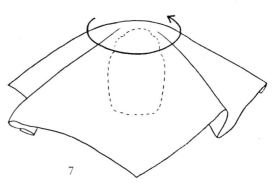

7

Secure the paper around the
lid of the jar with the wire or
string.

JAR A

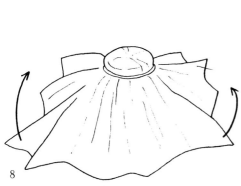

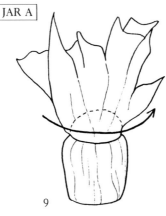

8

Gather the paper at the top
of the jar.

9

For Jar A: Gather the paper
and secure with wire or
string.

10

Spread the paper out above
the tied area.

JAR B

11

For Jar B: Gather the paper.
Twist it, then tie it in a knot.

These jar covers are adapted from the white cover secured with gold *mizuhiki* that once topped containers of the saké offered to the gods. Even now, certain traditional foods are sold with a paper cover secured with string, usually in addition to an ordinary lid.

Materials

GIFT
Jar of jam: 4½″(h)×2½″ (lid diameter), 2 jars

PAPER
Jar A: 7″(d) medium-weight light yellow washi, 6½″(d) medium-weight purple washi
Jar B: 6½″×6½″ medium-weight washi, 1 sheet of white and 1 of red, 2½″ × 2½″ cardboard

OTHER MATERIALS
Jar A: 22″ gold-and-brown cord
Jar B: 5 strands of 40″ mizuhiki (see page 68)

JAR A

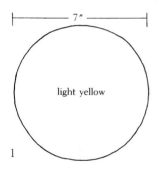

light yellow

1

purple

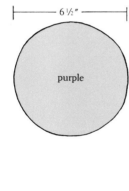

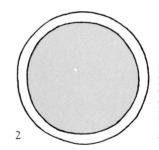

2

Glue the wrong side of the purple circle to the right side of the yellow. Make sure the centers are aligned. The purple should be on top, with a ¼″ yellow border running around the perimeter.

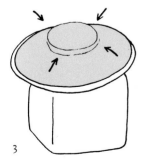

3

Place the paper on the lid of the jar and shape it around the lid.

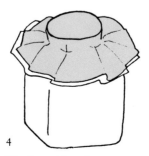

4

Tie the gold cord around the lid.

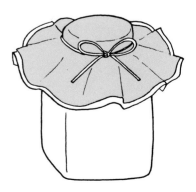

1

6½" white 6½"

6½" red 6½"

2½" cardboard
2½"

2

wrong side of white paper

wrong side of red paper

Place the red paper on top of the white to form an eight-point star as shown. Both sheets should be wrong side up. Fold to the right along a line drawn from the points where the edges meet.

3

½"

Leaving ½", fold this section back to the left.

4

½"

Repeat the same procedure with the opposite side.

5

Drawing a line between the points where the edges meet, fold the paper down.

6

½"

Leaving ½", fold the paper back up.

7

Fold up the bottom in the same way.

8

½"

Leaving ½", fold the paper down.

9

Crease all fold lines, then unfold completely.

10

cardboard

Glue the square of cardboard in the center.

11

Turn the paper over and place over the top of the jar.

12

Following the instructions given in Gift 3, tie the *mizuhiki* strands.

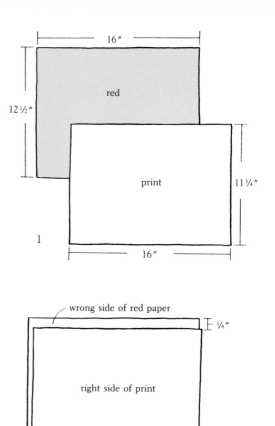

The use of a print adds an extra touch to this practical wrapping. Try a copy of your favorite drawing or painting or some vividly colored wrapping paper.

Materials

GIFT
Wine: 11¾″(h)×3″(d) bottle

PAPER
11¾″×16″ medium-weight washi print
12½″×16″ medium-weight red washi

OTHER MATERIALS
10 strands of 28″ white mizuhiki (see page 68)

Glue wrong sides of the print and the red sheet together. Leave a ¾″ strip of the red paper visible along the length of the print.

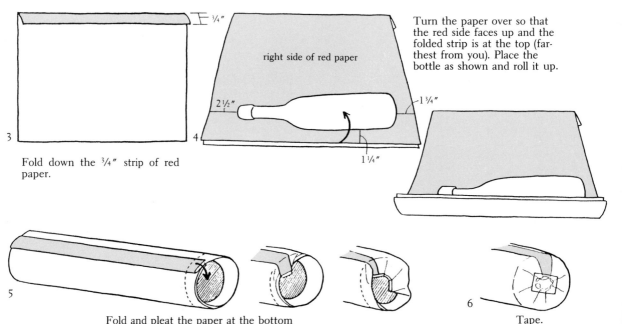

Fold down the ¾″ strip of red paper.

Turn the paper over so that the red side faces up and the folded strip is at the top (farthest from you). Place the bottle as shown and roll it up.

Fold and pleat the paper at the bottom of the bottle. Fold the red strip down first.

Tape.

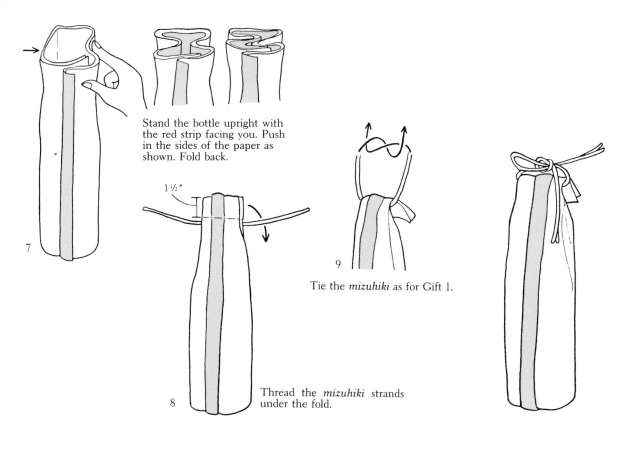

Stand the bottle upright with the red strip facing you. Push in the sides of the paper as shown. Fold back.

7

1 ½"

8

Thread the *mizuhiki* strands under the fold.

9

Tie the *mizuhiki* as for Gift 1.

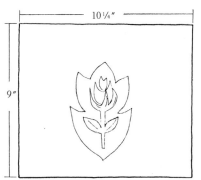

10 ¼"

9"

This wrapping is ideal when you are pressed for time. Try using a sticker or drawing on solid color paper.

Materials

GIFT
Wine: 11 ¼" (h) × 2 ¾" (d) bottle

PAPER
9" × 10 ¼" washi with a rose on it
Cut a printed sheet of paper to size or make your own.

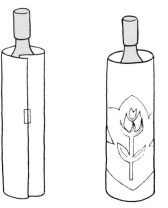

Wrap the paper around the wine bottle and tape it in place. If you are making your own paper, attach a sticker (or draw a picture) in the center of the paper.

22

The way this wrapping is turned back at the bottom reminds you of the glimpse of the colorful lining of the kimono that you get when a woman walks.

Materials

GIFT
Wine: 11¾″(h)×2¾″(d) bottle

PAPER
13¾″×17¾″ medium-weight brown-flecked ivory washi
13¾″×17½″ lightweight green washi
13¾″×17¼″ lightweight light blue washi

OTHER MATERIALS
27½″ of ½″ hemp ribbon

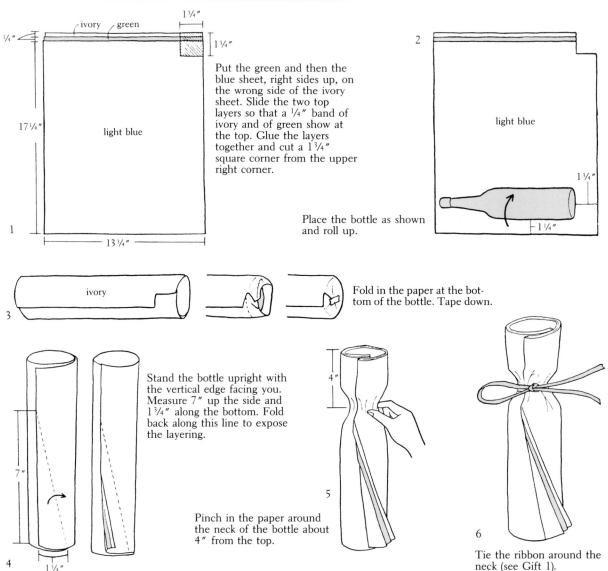

Put the green and then the blue sheet, right sides up, on the wrong side of the ivory sheet. Slide the two top layers so that a ¼″ band of ivory and of green show at the top. Glue the layers together and cut a 1¾″ square corner from the upper right corner.

Place the bottle as shown and roll up.

Fold in the paper at the bottom of the bottle. Tape down.

Stand the bottle upright with the vertical edge facing you. Measure 7″ up the side and 1¾″ along the bottom. Fold back along this line to expose the layering.

Pinch in the paper around the neck of the bottle about 4″ from the top.

Tie the ribbon around the neck (see Gift 1).

The best things come in small packages

One of these ideas should be just right when you wrap something small, like homemade candies or cookies, chocolates, potpourri, or even small accessories.

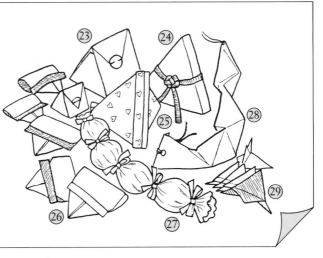

In the Meiji period (1868–1912), people reinforced these boxes with a layer of cloth and used them as purses. These light and roomy boxes can be used for a variety of gifts.

Materials

GIFT
Large box: *about 3″ (d) round item (such as candies or cookies wrapped in clear plastic)*
Small box: *about 1½″ (d) round item (candies, cookies, or jewelry)*

PAPER
Large box: *12″ × 14¾″ medium-weight shiny black paper*
Small box: *6″ × 7½″ medium-weight shiny red paper*

LARGE BOX

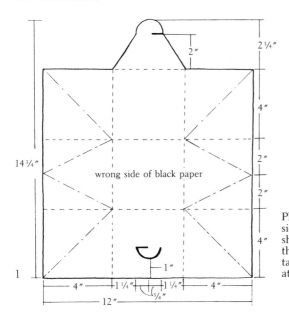

wrong side of black paper

14¾″

2″
2¾″
4″
2″
2″
4″

12″
4″ 1¼″ 1¼″ 4″
¾″
1″

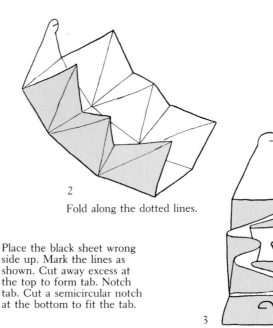

2
Fold along the dotted lines.

Place the black sheet wrong side up. Mark the lines as shown. Cut away excess at the top to form tab. Notch tab. Cut a semicircular notch at the bottom to fit the tab.

3
Slip the left and right folds into each other as shown.

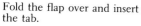

SMALL BOX

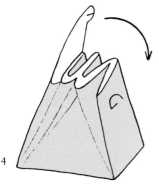

4 Fold the flap over and insert the tab.

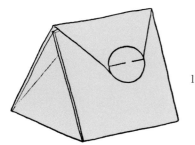

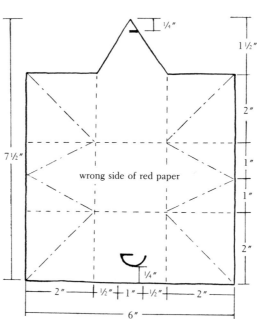

wrong side of red paper

¼"

1½"

2"

1"

1"

2"

7½"

1

2" ½" 1" ½" 2"

6"

¼"

Lay the red sheet wrong side up and mark as shown. Cut away excess paper at the top to form a triangular tab. Notch. Carefully measure, then cut a notch at the bottom.

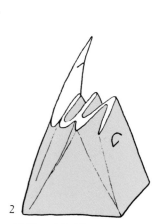

2 Fold and finish as instructed in steps 2 to 4 of the large box.

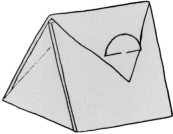

24

This wrapping was once used to package *natto*, fermented soybeans. Two triangles were used here, but you can use as many or as few as you like.

Materials

GIFT
Thin items (handkerchiefs) which will fit inside a 6" equilateral triangle

PAPER
5" × 18" medium-weight shiny paper, 2 sheets of red and white poinsettia print and 2 sheets of white

OTHER MATERIALS
34" of ¼" green ribbon

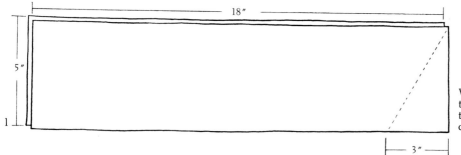

18"

5"

1

3"

With right sides out, glue the two sheets of poinsettia print together. Fold the lower right corner in. Insert gift.

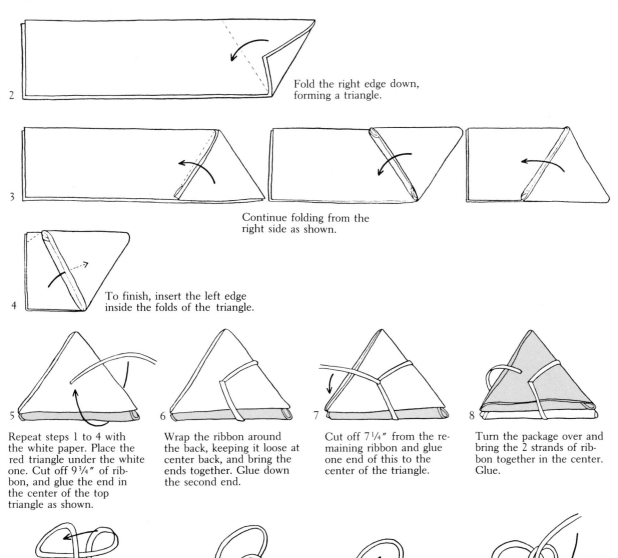

2 Fold the right edge down, forming a triangle.

3 Continue folding from the right side as shown.

4 To finish, insert the left edge inside the folds of the triangle.

5 Repeat steps 1 to 4 with the white paper. Place the red triangle under the white one. Cut off 9¾" of ribbon, and glue the end in the center of the top triangle as shown.

6 Wrap the ribbon around the back, keeping it loose at center back, and bring the ends together. Glue down the second end.

7 Cut off 7¼" from the remaining ribbon and glue one end of this to the center of the triangle.

8 Turn the package over and bring the 2 strands of ribbon together in the center. Glue.

9 Loop the ribbon as shown above.

10 Cross the right loop over the left loop. Pass the long end of the ribbon under the right ribbon.

11 Pass the long end through the loop as shown.

12 Pass both ends of the ribbon through the loop again.

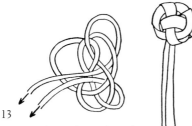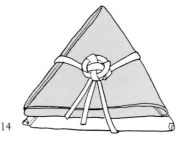

13 Pull gently on the ends and shape the bow as you go along.

14 Glue the bow to the center of the package.

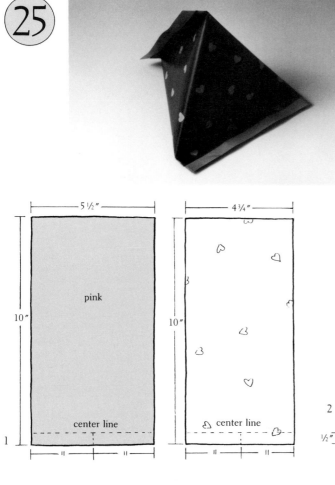

25

This type of pyramidlike package was first used in Sweden. In Japan, in addition to gift wrapping, it has found widespread acceptance as a small-scale carton for milk and other beverages.

Materials

GIFT
About 2″ (d) round item (such as cookies or candies wrapped in clear plastic)

PAPER
5½″ × 10″ medium-weight pink paper
4¾″ × 10″ medium-weight green-and-pink paper

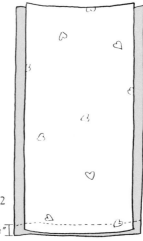

Place the green-and-pink sheet on top of the pink sheet, right sides up, matching center lines. Glue the layers together to prevent shifting.

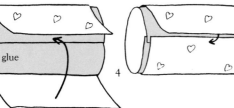

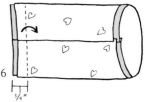

Roll into a tube, so that the ends overlap ½″. Glue the ends of the pink paper together first.

Glue the green-and-pink ends together.

Flatten one end of the tube so that the overlapped area is in the center of the flattened end.

Crease the outer edges and flatten the outer ¾″ of the tube.

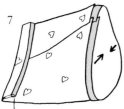

Fold in the flattened ¾″ strip and glue. Insert gift. Close up the other end of the tube by lifting the overlapped area up, bringing it to a point at the top of the wrapping, and pinching in the sides. Crease the edges.

Flatten ¾″ of the outer edge of the tube. Fold this ¾″ flap toward the front and glue.

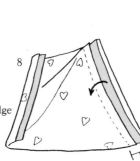

These little packets are handy for wrapping candies or cookies individually. Place little chocolate hearts, kisses, or other fanciful chocolates inside for children. Or use these packets to wrap jewelry or potpourri.

Materials

GIFT
About 1″ (d) candies or cookies

PAPER
3″ × 7″ lightweight washi *or tracing paper*
3″ × 7″ colored cellophane
(for one packet)

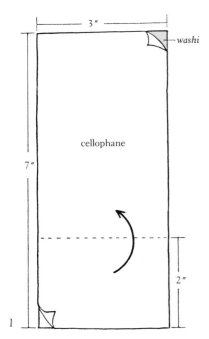

1

Place the thin sheet of cellophane over the sheet of *washi*, right side up. Fold the bottom 2″ up.

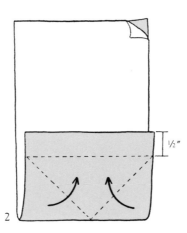

2

Leaving a ½″ strip at the top, fold up the lower corners so that they meet in the middle.

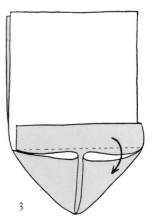

3

Fold down the ½″ strip.

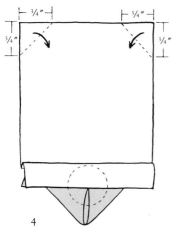

4

Put the gift inside. Fold down the upper corners.

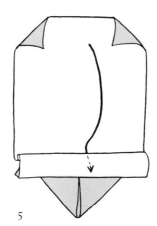

5

Insert the top flap into the folded triangle. Glue the sides of the flap down if desired.

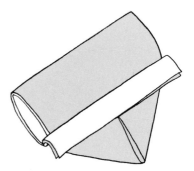

This creative package is a new and charming way to wrap golf balls or candy.

Materials

GIFT
1½" (d) balls, 4

PAPER
9¾" × 14½" lightweight yellow washi, 2 sheets

OTHER MATERIALS
5 strands of 9¾" long ¼" red ribbon
String

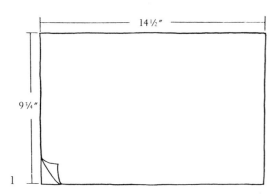

1 Place one sheet on top of the other, wrong sides together. (Using two sheets adds strength and makes the ends of the wrapping attractive.) Trim the short sides with pinking shears.

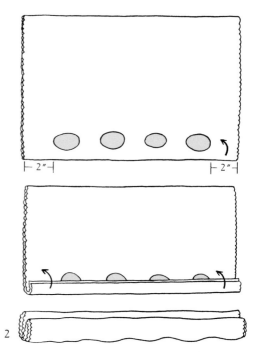

2 Leaving 2" of paper at each end, space the balls evenly, and then wrap the balls by slowly rolling up the paper.

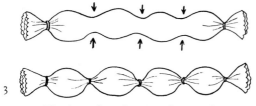

3 Tie the ends with string, then tie the gaps between the balls.

4 Tie the red ribbons over the string.

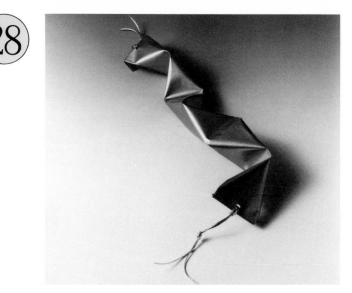

Washi can be folded to produce varied and complex patterns. The same pinching technique that produces this silver snake makes a tortoiseshell pattern when unfolded.

Materials

GIFT
Small pieces of candy

PAPER
11" × 18" medium-weight silver metallic paper

OTHER MATERIALS
2 strands of 14" silver cord
Double-faced tape

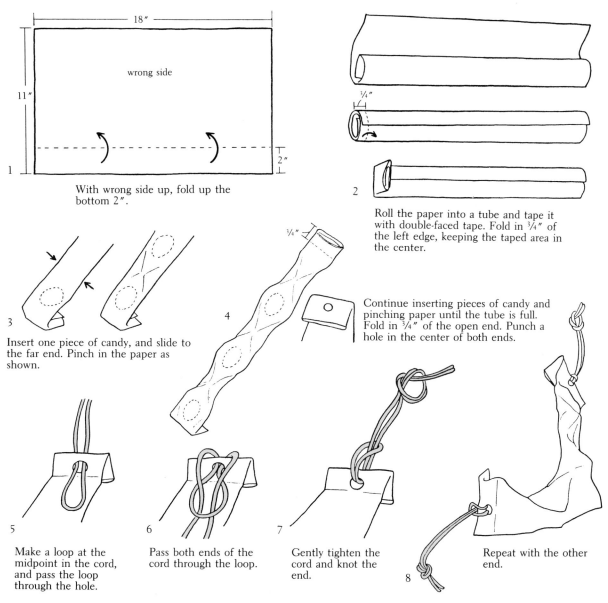

1 With wrong side up, fold up the bottom 2".

2 Roll the paper into a tube and tape it with double-faced tape. Fold in ¾" of the left edge, keeping the taped area in the center.

3 Insert one piece of candy, and slide to the far end. Pinch in the paper as shown.

4 Continue inserting pieces of candy and pinching paper until the tube is full. Fold in ¾" of the open end. Punch a hole in the center of both ends.

5 Make a loop at the midpoint in the cord, and pass the loop through the hole.

6 Pass both ends of the cord through the loop.

7 Gently tighten the cord and knot the end.

8 Repeat with the other end.

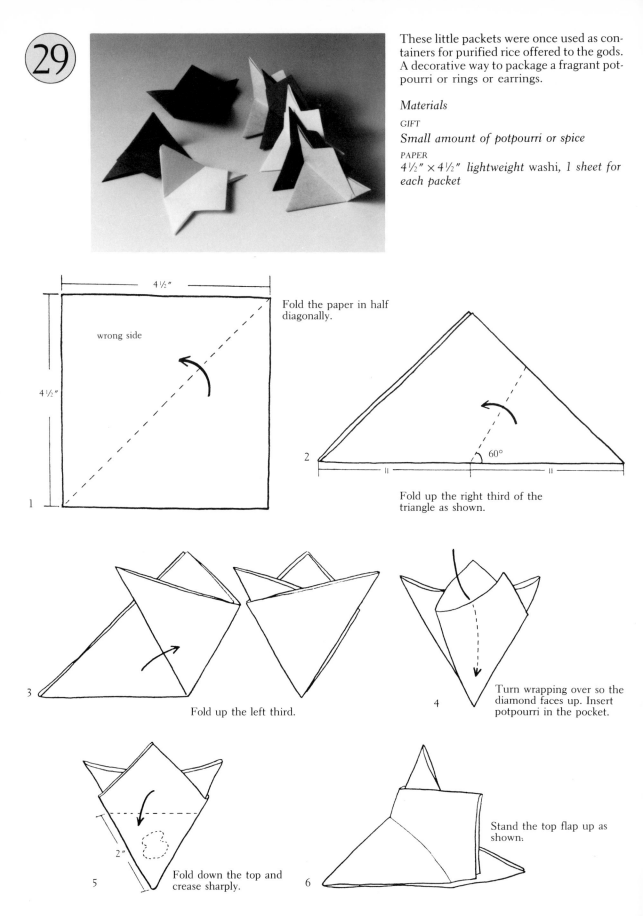

These little packets were once used as containers for purified rice offered to the gods. A decorative way to package a fragrant potpourri or rings or earrings.

Materials

GIFT
Small amount of potpourri or spice

PAPER
$4\frac{1}{2}" \times 4\frac{1}{2}"$ *lightweight* washi, *1 sheet for each packet*

4 ½"

wrong side

4 ½"

1

Fold the paper in half diagonally.

2

60°

Fold up the right third of the triangle as shown.

3

Fold up the left third.

4

Turn wrapping over so the diamond faces up. Insert potpourri in the pocket.

5

2"

Fold down the top and crease sharply.

6

Stand the top flap up as shown.

Flowers and plants

Very traditional Japanese shapes and very traditional colors—red and white—are used to create lively wrappings for flowers and potted plants. Coordinate the color of the paper with the color of the flower or plant.

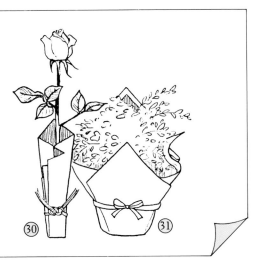

㉚ ㉛

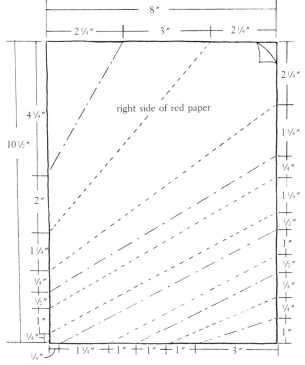

This unusual and eye-catching shape is a traditional Japanese wrapping for a flower.

Materials

GIFT
15″ *red rose (or any flower)*

PAPER
8″ × 10½″ *heavyweight white* washi
8″ × 10½″ *medium-weight red* washi

OTHER MATERIALS
5 *strands of 13¾″ red-and-white* mizuhiki *(see page 68)*

1

right side of red paper

Glue wrong sides together. Score or mark paper. (Or make a practice sheet of the same size. Score, mark, and fold it, then lay it on top of the red side and use its fold lines as a guide.)

2

With the red side facing up, crease as indicated.

3

Following the fold lines, fold in the left edge, then fold up the right edge and place it over the left edge.

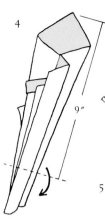

4

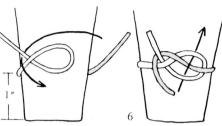

Measure 9″ from the top and tuck the bottom part under. Insert flower.

9″

5

1″

Place *mizuhiki* strands about 1″ from the bottom. Make a loop with the white (left) end as shown and pass the red end under the upper white strand and over the lower one.

6

Weave the red end through the white loop in an under-over-under pattern as shown.

7

Gently pull the ends to adjust and shape, until the *mizuhiki* bow is symmetrical and the ends are even.

(31)

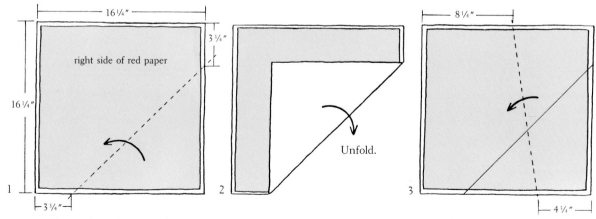

This wrapping is also a traditional Japanese wrapping for flowers and plants. Here it has been used to wrap a potted plant. Experiment with plants in baskets and with ordinary gift wrap and ribbons.

Materials

GIFT
Potted plant (dimensions of pot):
2¾″(h) × 4¼″ (diameter of bottom)

PAPER
16¼″ × 16¼″ medium-weight white washi
15½″ × 15½″ medium-weight red washi

OTHER MATERIAL
35″ of ½″ gold ribbon
Compass

16¼″

right side of red paper

3¾″

16¼″

1

3¾″

Center the red paper right side up on the wrong side of the white sheet. Glue together in the center to prevent slipping. Fold the lower right corner up as shown.

2

Unfold.

8¼″

3

4¼″

Fold the right edge in as shown.

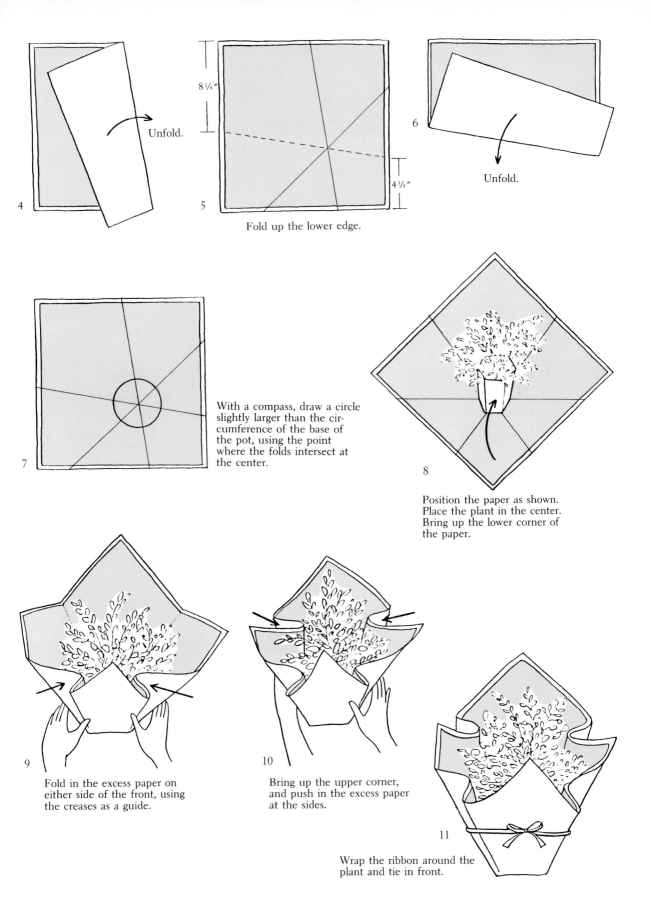

Unfold.

8 ¼"

4 ¾"

6

Unfold.

4

5

Fold up the lower edge.

With a compass, draw a circle slightly larger than the circumference of the base of the pot, using the point where the folds intersect at the center.

7

8

Position the paper as shown. Place the plant in the center. Bring up the lower corner of the paper.

9

Fold in the excess paper on either side of the front, using the creases as a guide.

10

Bring up the upper corner, and push in the excess paper at the sides.

11

Wrap the ribbon around the plant and tie in front.

Mizuhiki

Mizuhiki *are dyed paper cords for gift wrapping. Attaching a cord to a package and knotting it has the ob-
vious practical function of securing the wrapping. But
in Japan it also has the important symbolic function
of preventing impurities from entering the package.
Once tied,* mizuhiki *lose their starchy resilience and
cannot be tied again—thus* mizuhiki *are used some-
what like a wax seal in the West. Remember this
aspect of Japanese etiquette and avoid reusing* mizuhiki.

In the beginning of the seventh century, Ono no Imo-
ko, a court official and diplomat, led an embassy to
China. He returned with numerous goodwill gifts, some
tied with red-and-white cords.* Mizuhiki *are thought to
have developed from these cords. These early ties were
made of twisted paper and known as* koyori. *Later,
after the discovery that starching the cords made them
stronger and more pliable,* koyori *began to be used in
many different ways. Subsequently, the varieties of*
koyori—*the number of strands, the colors, the lengths,
etc.—began to proliferate, and the forms known as*
mizuhiki *were developed.*

Today there are eight color types of* mizuhiki: *crimson and white, for very formal occasions; red and white,
for general use and auspicious occasions; gold and silver,
for general use, though mainly for weddings and other
auspicious occasions; red and gold, used in the same
way as red and white; multi-colored, for informal decorative use; black and white, blue and white, and white,
all for funerals and condolences.*

Mizuhiki *come in many thicknesses—five-strand,
seven-strand, nine-strand, eleven-strand, etc.—but the
five-strand variety is most common. The length varies
from about eighteen inches to almost six feet.*

The way the* mizuhiki *are tied is also determined by
the occasion. For weddings and tragic occasions such
as funerals—events that are never to be repeated
again—the* musubikiri *(flat knot) method is used. This
knot cannot be untied, symbolizing that what has hap-
pened will not happen again. At auspicious times (other
than weddings) the* katawana-musubi *or* morowana-
musubi *(types of bows) are generally used. Though informal, the detached* awabi-musubi *(abalone knot) is
also popular. Wrapping the end of the* mizuhiki *around
and around represents waves breaking on the shore. This
method is used for happy occasions. The* gyaku *(reverse)*
awabi-musubi *is used only for Buddhist memorial ser-
vices and other solemn events.*

Whatever knot is being used, begin tying with the
white or paler color cords on the left side. Cross them
over the darker color on the right.* Mizuhiki *are easily
damaged or broken, so it is probably best to estimate
where the knot will be before tying. Gently work that
area with the fingers to soften the strands slightly, or
steam them for a moment to achieve the same effect.*
Mizuhiki, *as stated before, cannot be retied, so it is best
to practice first.*

Various grades of* washi *are used for making these
twisted cords. The cords are made by cutting one-fourth-
to one-half-inch strips of paper and twisting them.
Traditionally, the cord was soaked in the starchy water
left from washing rice. It was then removed from the
water, the excess water wiped away, and the cord left
to dry in the sun.* Mizuhiki *are now made by machine.
Starch is applied and spread evenly in one direction.
The cord is heat dried and then dyed and cut.*

HOW TO MAKE MIZUHIKI

When* mizuhiki *are not available, try making your
own with crochet cotton (heavier weight) and gesso. Cut
as many strands of crochet cotton as you need, each
approximately one inch longer than the length needed. Thin the gesso until it is about the consistency of
whipping cream. White crochet cotton can be dyed light
colors by dissolving poster colors in the gesso. Place the
crochet cotton in the gesso or apply the gesso with a
brush. Stretch the strands out straight and pin or tape
the ends to keep the strands in place. Let dry for over
an hour.*

The gifts in this book that use* mizuhiki *are 1, 3, 7,
11, 13, 15, 19, 20, 30, 45, and 53.*

Mizuhiki variations (from left to right): Awabi-musubi, same knot with decorative crane, musubikiri, same knot with curled ends, morowana-musubi, gyaku awabi-musubi.

FLATLAND

*Here in Flatland find the perfect wrapping
for concert or theater tickets, records,
children's books, or photographs.*

Long and narrow

Squares
see page 76, Gifts 35–39

Flowers
see page 83, Gifts 40–43

Long and narrow

These three traditional Japanese wrappings are perfect for concert and theater tickets or photographs. Or use one as an envelope for a card.

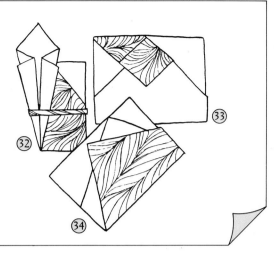

This wrapping is actually a chopstick holder for special festive occasions. There are two spaces in which to put things: the right front pocket where the chopsticks traditionally go and the pocket behind this. A diamond-shaped *noshi* (see Gift 12) decorates the holder.

Materials

GIFT
2½″ × 5″ flat item (tickets, photographs)

PAPER
10″ × 10″ lightweight white washi or tracing paper
5″ triangle of medium-weight marbled paper
¼″ × 7″ strip of medium-weight marbled paper

1
With the wrong side face up, fold the white square in half diagonally.

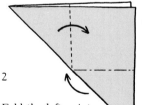

2
Fold the left point over to the right and the bottom point under, forming a square, with a triangular flap on each side.

3
Turn the square on its side so the triangular flap on the top points down and the folded edge of the flap is at the top. Lift up the triangular flap.

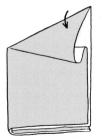

4
Open and flatten the triangle, centering it.

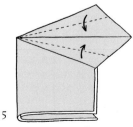

5
Fold edges to the center.

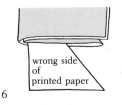

6
Insert the colored triangle, right side down, into the triangular flap on the underside of the square.

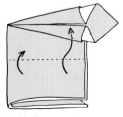

7
Fold the square area in half, and hide the edge under the diamond shaped *noshi*.

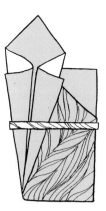

8

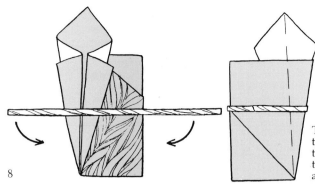

Turn the wrapping around so the *noshi* is on the left. Wrap the ¼″ strip of paper around the front of the wrapping, and glue on at the back.

③③

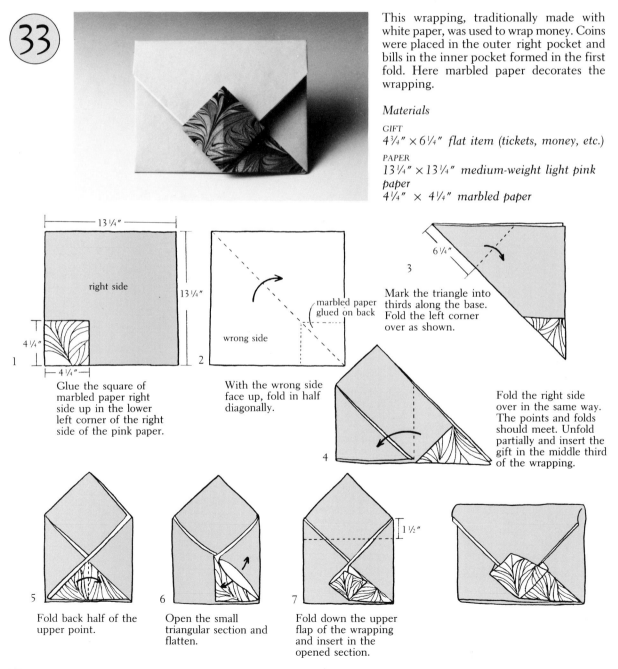

This wrapping, traditionally made with white paper, was used to wrap money. Coins were placed in the outer right pocket and bills in the inner pocket formed in the first fold. Here marbled paper decorates the wrapping.

Materials

GIFT
4¾″ × 6¼″ *flat item (tickets, money, etc.)*
PAPER
13¼″ × 13¼″ *medium-weight light pink paper*
4¼″ × 4¼″ *marbled paper*

1

— 13¼″ —

right side

13¼″

4¼″

— 4¼″ —

Glue the square of marbled paper right side up in the lower left corner of the right side of the pink paper.

2

wrong side

marbled paper glued on back

With the wrong side face up, fold in half diagonally.

3

6¼″

Mark the triangle into thirds along the base. Fold the left corner over as shown.

4

Fold the right side over in the same way. The points and folds should meet. Unfold partially and insert the gift in the middle third of the wrapping.

5

Fold back half of the upper point.

6

Open the small triangular section and flatten.

7

1½″

Fold down the upper flap of the wrapping and insert in the opened section.

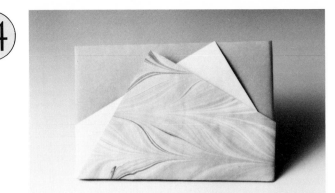

This eye-catching packet was originally used to give facial powder as a wedding present. Since both the front and back of the paper are utilized to create this effect, reversible paper or two sheets of paper glued back to back should be used.

Materials

GIFT
4" × 5½" *flat item (tickets, photographs)*

PAPER
9¾" × 13¼" *medium-weight light blue paper (white on wrong side)*
5¼" × 9¾" *triangle of medium-weight marbled paper*

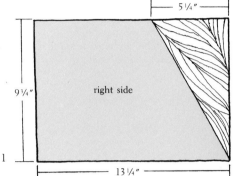

Glue the triangle of marbled paper, right side up, in the upper right corner of the right side of the light blue paper.

Turn the paper over so the point of the triangle is at upper left. Fold the right edge of the paper to the left along the line indicated.

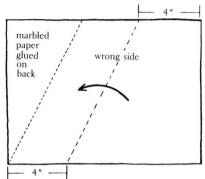

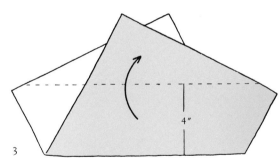

Measure 4" from the fold, and fold again.

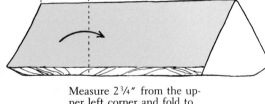

Measure 2¾" from the upper left corner and fold to the right. Unfold and insert the gift between the two layers of paper. Slide the gift to the left. Fold again.

Measure 2½" from the upper right corner and to the left.

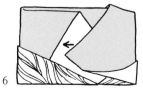

Insert the right end into the fold of the left end.

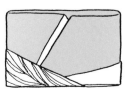

Back of the wrapping.

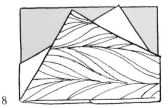

Front of the wrapping.

Squares

Wrapping the perfect square can be as exciting and new as these five ideas.

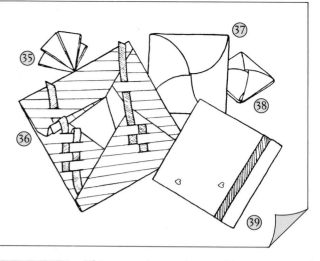

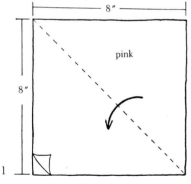

35

This unusual wrapping combines two pieces of *origami*, Japanese paper folding. Try leaving the center slightly open so a tiny bit of the present can be seen.

Materials

GIFT
4" × 4" flat item (card, or enlarge the wrapping for a record)

PAPER
*8" × 8" medium-weight paper,
2 sheets of pink, 2 sheets of green*

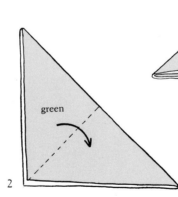

1.
8"
8"
pink

Glue each sheet of pink to a green sheet, back to back. With the pink side face up, fold the paper in half diagonally.

2. green

Fold in half again.

3.

Open the upper triangle.

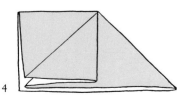

4.

Flatten into a square.

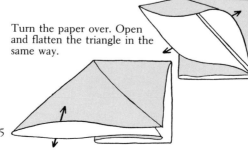

5.

Turn the paper over. Open and flatten the triangle in the same way.

6.

Fold up half of the top layer of the square.

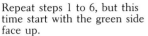

pink

7

Repeat steps 1 to 6, but this time start with the green side face up.

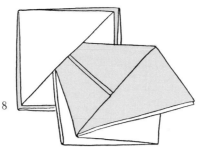

8

Insert the gift in the pocket made in step 7 of one square and slide this square into the other.

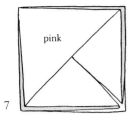

36

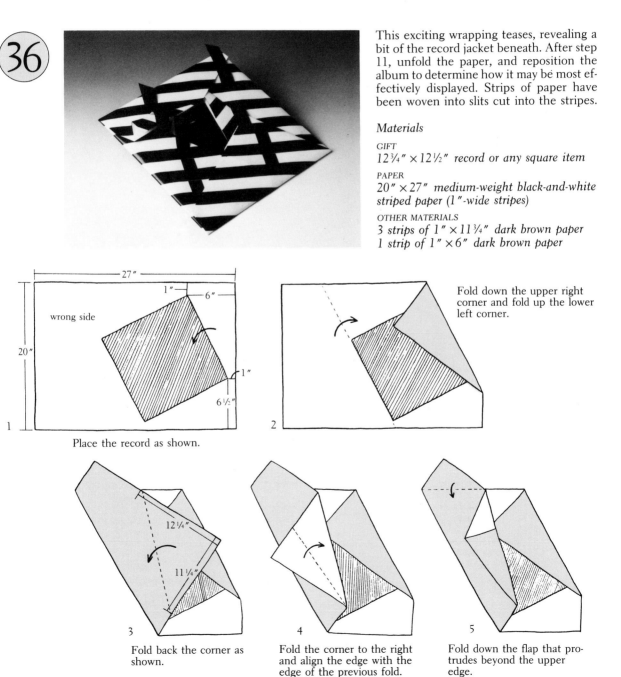

This exciting wrapping teases, revealing a bit of the record jacket beneath. After step 11, unfold the paper, and reposition the album to determine how it may be most effectively displayed. Strips of paper have been woven into slits cut into the stripes.

Materials

GIFT
12¾″ × 12½″ *record or any square item*

PAPER
20″ × 27″ *medium-weight black-and-white striped paper (1″-wide stripes)*

OTHER MATERIALS
3 strips of 1″ × 11¾″ dark brown paper
1 strip of 1″ × 6″ dark brown paper

27″

1″   6″

wrong side

20″

1″

6½″

1

Place the record as shown.

2

Fold down the upper right corner and fold up the lower left corner.

12¼″

11¼″

3

Fold back the corner as shown.

4

Fold the corner to the right and align the edge with the edge of the previous fold.

5

Fold down the flap that protrudes beyond the upper edge.

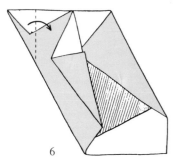

6

Fold the upper corner in at a right angle to the upper edge.

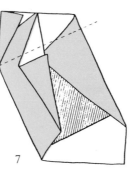

7

Fold the upper section over the record, using the record edge as a guide.

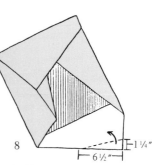

8

1¼"

6½"

Fold up a portion of the bottom right corner as shown.

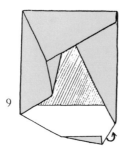

9

Fold the small triangular section under.

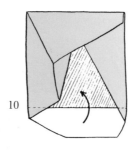

10

Fold the lower section over the album along the edge of the record.

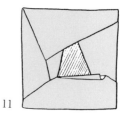

11

Rotate the package 180°.

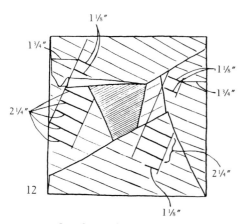

1⅛"

1¾"

2¼"

2¼"

1⅛"

1⅛"

1¾"

12

Cut slits in the paper, using the stripes as a guide. Place a piece of protective cardboard under the paper to protect the record when you cut.

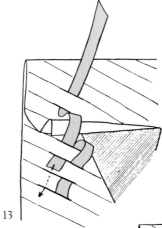

13

Weave the strips of paper through the slits. The short strip is for the lower right side.

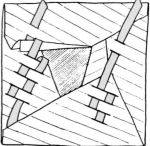

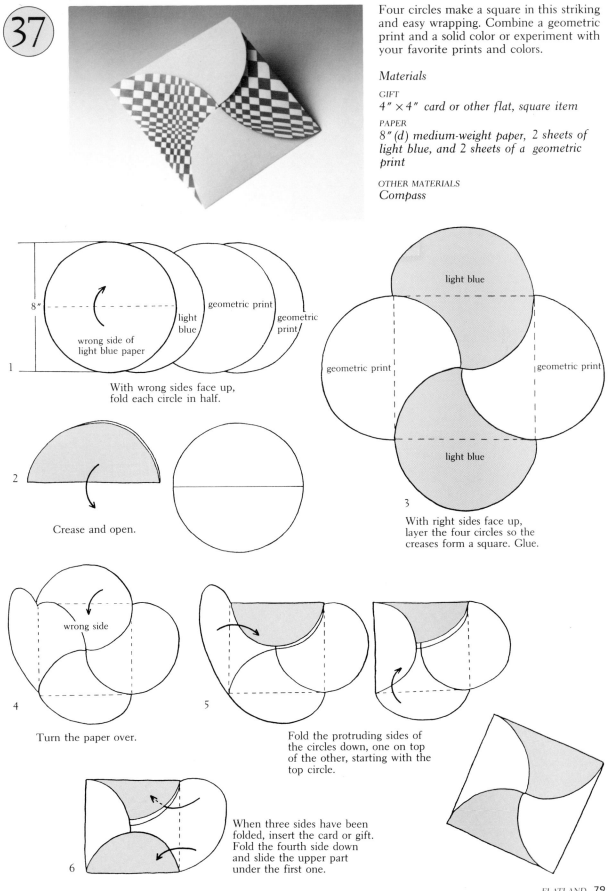

37

Four circles make a square in this striking and easy wrapping. Combine a geometric print and a solid color or experiment with your favorite prints and colors.

Materials

GIFT
4″ × 4″ card or other flat, square item

PAPER
8″ (d) medium-weight paper, 2 sheets of light blue, and 2 sheets of a geometric print

OTHER MATERIALS
Compass

1 8″ — wrong side of light blue paper — light blue — geometric print — geometric print

With wrong sides face up, fold each circle in half.

2 Crease and open.

3 light blue — geometric print — geometric print — light blue

With right sides face up, layer the four circles so the creases form a square. Glue.

4 wrong side

Turn the paper over.

5 Fold the protruding sides of the circles down, one on top of the other, starting with the top circle.

6 When three sides have been folded, insert the card or gift. Fold the fourth side down and slide the upper part under the first one.

This folded pinwheel was adapted from the *origami* pinwheel. This interesting wrapping has two places where a gift can be inserted.

Materials

GIFT
4″ × 4″ *card or other flat, square item*
PAPER
12″ × 12″ *medium-weight printed paper, 1 sheet of orange and 1 sheet of blue*

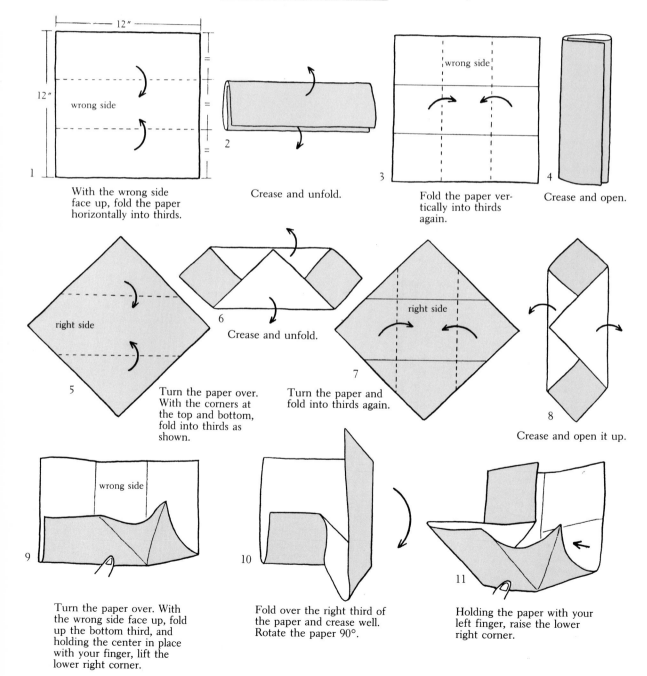

With the wrong side face up, fold the paper horizontally into thirds.

Crease and unfold.

Fold the paper vertically into thirds again.

Crease and open.

Turn the paper over. With the corners at the top and bottom, fold into thirds as shown.

Crease and unfold.

Turn the paper and fold into thirds again.

Crease and open it up.

Turn the paper over. With the wrong side face up, fold up the bottom third, and holding the center in place with your finger, lift the lower right corner.

Fold over the right third of the paper and crease well. Rotate the paper 90°.

Holding the paper with your left finger, raise the lower right corner.

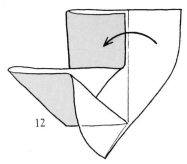

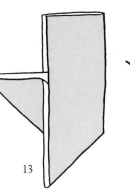

12

Fold the right third of the paper over the center, making the lower right corner come out in a point on the bottom.

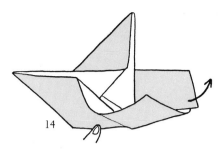

13

Rotate the paper 90°.

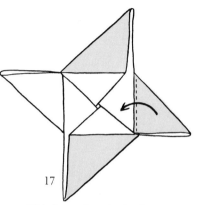

14

Holding the paper with your left finger, lift up the top corner and bring it down. Still holding the top corner, lift the bottom corner and pull upward.

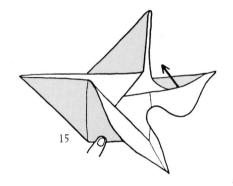

15

Flatten the paper so that one corner points down and the other up.

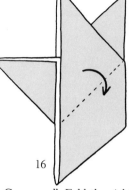

16

Crease well. Fold the right-hand point over and downward.

17

This forms the pinwheel. Fold in the right wing of the pinwheel.

18   Fold the bottom wing over the right wing.

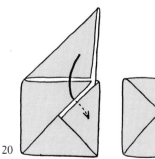

19

Fold the left wing over the bottom wing.

20

Fold the top wing over and insert the point under the bottommost wing.

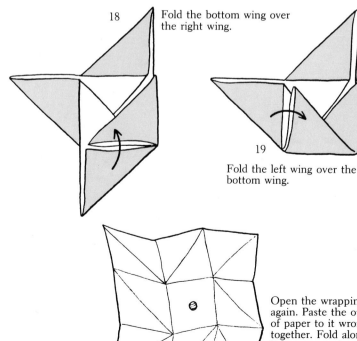

21

Open the wrapping once again. Paste the other sheet of paper to it wrong sides together. Fold along the fold lines once again. Insert the gift after step 16 or insert the gift at step 9.

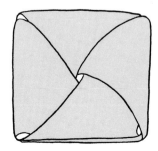

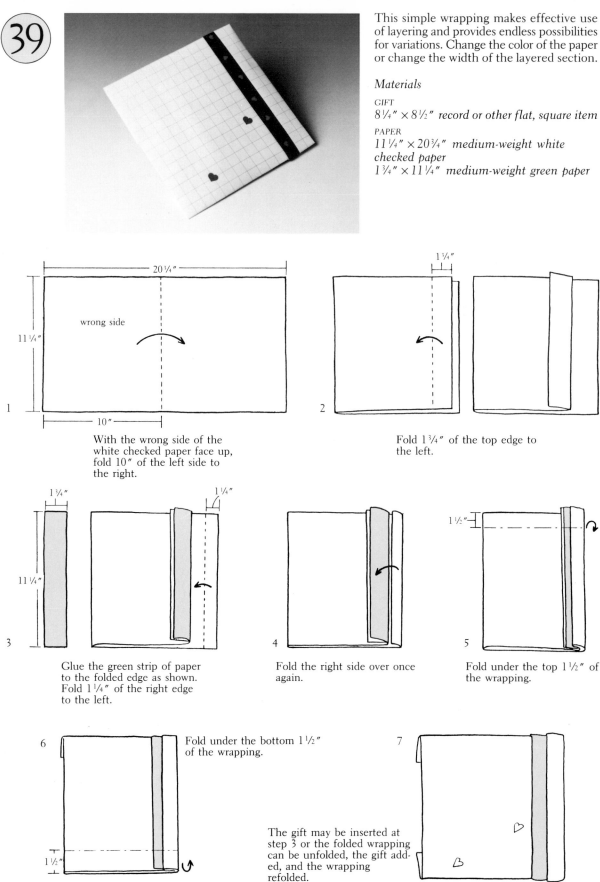

39

This simple wrapping makes effective use of layering and provides endless possibilities for variations. Change the color of the paper or change the width of the layered section.

Materials

GIFT
$8\,1/4'' \times 8\,1/2''$ *record or other flat, square item*

PAPER
$11\,1/4'' \times 20\,3/4''$ *medium-weight white checked paper*
$1\,3/4'' \times 11\,1/4''$ *medium-weight green paper*

1 — $20\,3/4''$ — $11\,1/4''$ — wrong side — $10''$

With the wrong side of the white checked paper face up, fold 10″ of the left side to the right.

2 — $1\,3/4''$

Fold $1\,3/4''$ of the top edge to the left.

3 — $1\,3/4''$ — $11\,1/4''$ — $1\,1/4''$

Glue the green strip of paper to the folded edge as shown. Fold $1\,1/4''$ of the right edge to the left.

4

Fold the right side over once again.

5 — $1\,1/2''$

Fold under the top $1\,1/2''$ of the wrapping.

6 — $1\,1/2''$

Fold under the bottom $1\,1/2''$ of the wrapping.

7

The gift may be inserted at step 3 or the folded wrapping can be unfolded, the gift added, and the wrapping refolded.

Flowers

This basic shape existed in the Edo period (1600–1868) and was used to hold thread and needles. All of the variations share the idea of twisting and folding the paper and of using both the right and wrong sides in the final design.

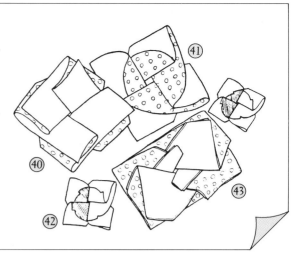

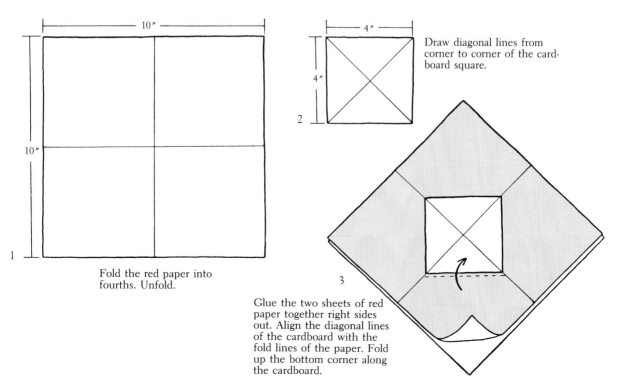

This wrapping, probably the most basic of the flower designs, is made by folding a square of paper around a square of cardboard.

Materials

GIFT
4″ × 4″ card or other flat, square item

PAPER
10″ × 10″ lightweight paper, red with purple polka dots, 2 sheets
4″ × 4″ cardboard

1 Fold the red paper into fourths. Unfold.

2 Draw diagonal lines from corner to corner of the cardboard square.

3 Glue the two sheets of red paper together right sides out. Align the diagonal lines of the cardboard with the fold lines of the paper. Fold up the bottom corner along the cardboard.

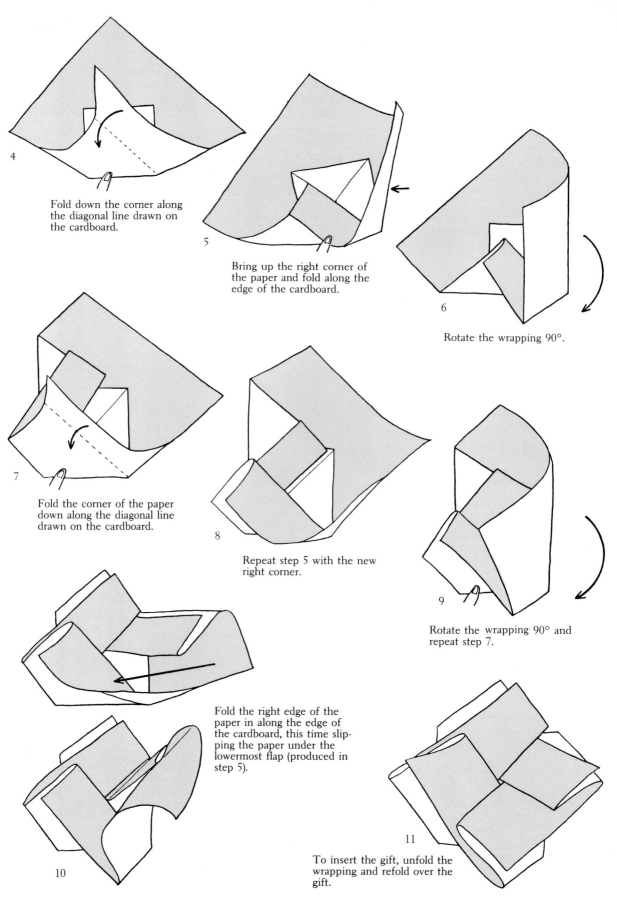

4

Fold down the corner along
the diagonal line drawn on
the cardboard.

5

Bring up the right corner of
the paper and fold along the
edge of the cardboard.

6

Rotate the wrapping 90°.

7

Fold the corner of the paper
down along the diagonal line
drawn on the cardboard.

8

Repeat step 5 with the new
right corner.

9

Rotate the wrapping 90° and
repeat step 7.

10

Fold the right edge of the
paper in along the edge of
the cardboard, this time slipping the paper under the
lowermost flap (produced in
step 5).

11

To insert the gift, unfold the
wrapping and refold over the
gift.

In this variation of the basic flower shape, the square of Gift 40 has been cut into a circle.

Materials

GIFT
$4\frac{1}{4}'' \times 4\frac{1}{4}''$ card or other flat, square item
PAPER
$12''$(d) medium-weight paper,
1 sheet of black with white polka dots and
1 sheet of white with black polka dots
$4\frac{1}{4}'' \times 4\frac{1}{4}''$ cardboard

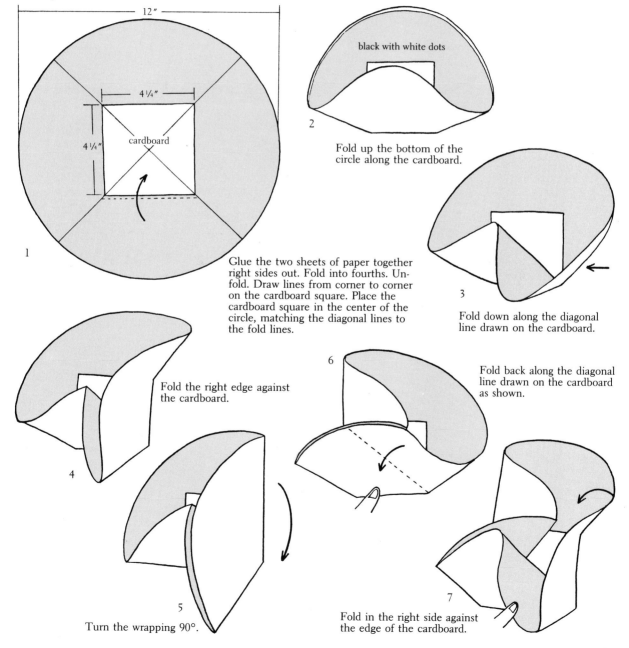

1

12"

4¼"

4¼"

cardboard

Glue the two sheets of paper together right sides out. Fold into fourths. Unfold. Draw lines from corner to corner on the cardboard square. Place the cardboard square in the center of the circle, matching the diagonal lines to the fold lines.

black with white dots

2

Fold up the bottom of the circle along the cardboard.

3

Fold down along the diagonal line drawn on the cardboard.

4

Fold the right edge against the cardboard.

5

Turn the wrapping 90°.

6

Fold back along the diagonal line drawn on the cardboard as shown.

7

Fold in the right side against the edge of the cardboard.

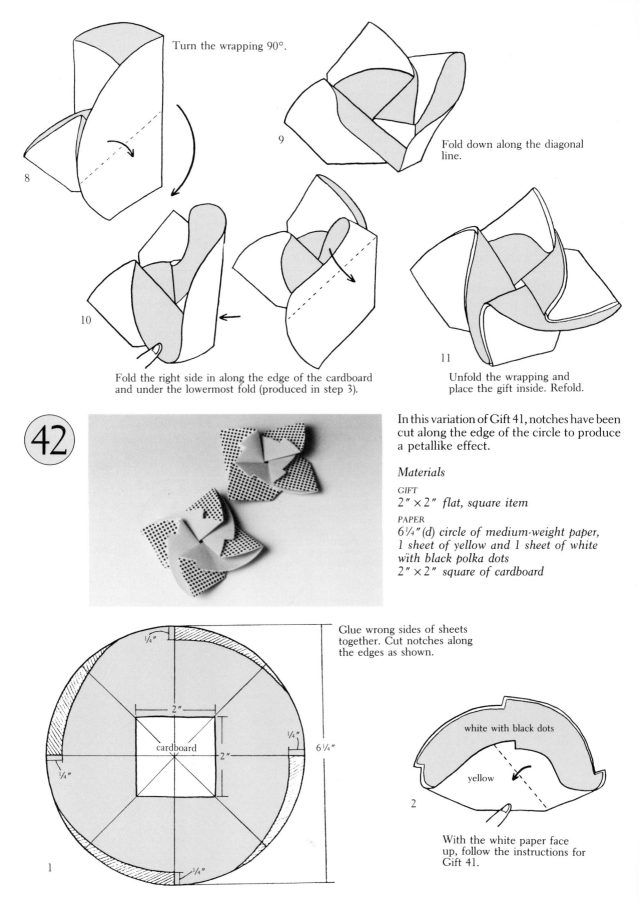

Turn the wrapping 90°.

8

9

Fold down along the diagonal line.

10

Fold the right side in along the edge of the cardboard and under the lowermost fold (produced in step 3).

11

Unfold the wrapping and place the gift inside. Refold.

42

In this variation of Gift 41, notches have been cut along the edge of the circle to produce a petallike effect.

Materials

GIFT
2″ × 2″ flat, square item

PAPER
6¼″ (d) circle of medium-weight paper, 1 sheet of yellow and 1 sheet of white with black polka dots
2″ × 2″ square of cardboard

Glue wrong sides of sheets together. Cut notches along the edges as shown.

¼″

2″

cardboard

2″

¼″

¼″

¼″

6¼″

1

white with black dots

yellow

2

With the white paper face up, follow the instructions for Gift 41.

43

This intriguing flower design can be adapted to wrap a rectangular gift. Experiment with colors and prints.

Materials

GIFT
4¾" × 7" *card or other flat item*

PAPER
11¾" × 11¾" *medium-weight paper,*
1 sheet of gray with white polka dots and
1 sheet of pink
4¾" × 7" *cardboard*

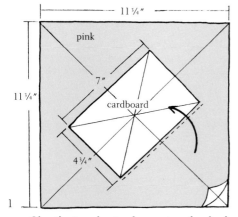

1

Glue the two sheets of paper together back to back. With the pink side up, fold the paper into fourths diagonally. Unfold. Draw lines on the cardboard as shown. Place the cardboard on the paper, matching the lines to the folds.

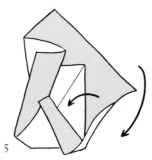

2

Fold up the bottom corner along the cardboard.

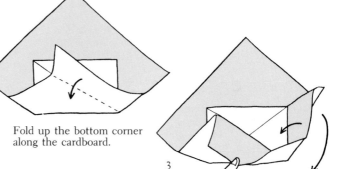

3

Fold back the edge and align along the diagonal line drawn on the cardboard. Fold up the right edge along the cardboard. Turn the wrapping 90°.

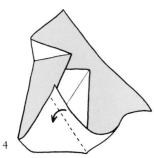

4

Fold back the edge and align along the diagonal line on the cardboard.

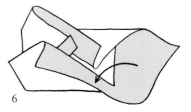

5

Fold up the right side along the cardboard. Turn the wrapping 90°.

6

Fold back along the diagonal line of the cardboard. Fold the last side in.

7

Slide the excess paper under the lowermost fold (produced in step 3).

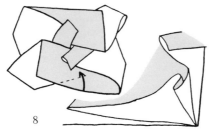

8

Fold the flaps of paper protruding past the corners of the cardboard toward the inside of the wrapping as shown.

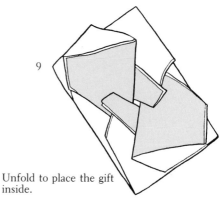

9

Unfold to place the gift inside.

Layering and Color

From the Nara period (710–794) to the beginning of the Heian period (794–1185), when China had a strong influence on Japanese culture, the clear, bright colors of the continent enjoyed great popularity. Later in the Heian period, however, tastes began to shift away from the Chinese aesthetic, and a characteristically Japanese culture was born. This shift in tastes was reflected in new forms of literature and art as well as major changes in color aesthetics. Subtle, neutral tones, drawn from the landscape around Kyoto, the Heian capital, became the favored colors.

The fascination with these rich neutral tones took the form of kasane no irome or layering of colors. Kasane no irome is the art of layering two or more colors, and it achieves its highest form in the layering of kimono which are worn one on top of the other in various thicknesses. A fine sensibility was needed to achieve a delicate harmony in combining the varied colors, patterns, and textures of materials.

Kasane no irome were given elegant names (usually those of flowers or plants), and kimono in these colors were worn at specified times of the year. When the kasane no irome was named after a flower, these colors were worn before and during the flower's blossoming, never after. For example, ume-gasane (plum blossom), outer layer: white, inner: crimson, was worn from November to February; fuji-gasane (wisteria), outer: light-purple, inner: blue, was worn in April; kikyō-gasane (gentian/bellflower), outer: pale lavender, inner: blue, was worn in August; and tsubaki-gasane (camellia), outer: purplish red, inner: red, was worn from October to December. This is only a small selection— there are many others: yanagi-gasane (willow), sakura-

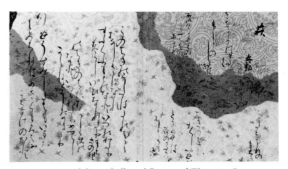

Two-page spread from *Collected Poems of Thirty-six Poets*.

gasane (cherry), waka kaede (young maple), aoi (hollyhock), momiji (red maple), ochiguri (fallen chestnut), koori (ice), and so on. Each has its own outer-layer and inner-layer colors. Then and now, people who wear kimono follow these strictures, bringing out new garments in just the right shades at the first sign of a change of season. Nor are all the kasane no irome limited to two-color combinations; there are rules governing tricolor groupings as well.

Kasane no irome is most evident in the choice of kimono, but it has also had significant influence in other areas, notably in traditional crafts. The art of Japanese bookmaking is a good example. The sixteenth-century waka poetry collection known as Sanjūroku-nin kashū (Collected Poems of Thirty-six Poets), a masterpiece of bookmaking, incorporates a variety of techniques based on kasane no irome. Parts of the book consist of strips of beautiful paper pieced together. In some sections, five sheets of thin paper, dyed to fade from a dark to a pale shade, have been layered on one another. In other places, the ends of the paper have been shifted slightly to create an effect similar to the rings of a tree. The edge of the layered paper is sometimes torn to make the color change soft and subtle, and sometimes cut in a straight line, making a sharper change. The patterns in this book have continued to have a strong influence on modern Japanese design.

There are three basic ways to create layers of color in gift wrapping. Use reversible paper or glue two sheets of paper together back to back to create inner and outer colors, and fold back the paper to reveal the inner color. Or layer two or more sheets of paper on top of each other. Begin with darker colors and work toward lighter ones, leaving some of the edge of each sheet exposed. Or place thinner or more transparent paper on the outside to let the color and design of the inner layer show through. Try using thin washi or crepe paper over colorful paper.

Experiment with various techniques. Solid-colored paper is only one possibility; use printed paper or other materials (cloth, plastic, cardboard, etc.). Try cutting the edge of the paper with a pinking shears or folding, crumpling, and creasing the paper to achieve a variety of textures.

The gifts in this book that use layering are 1, 4, 5, 6, 8, 13, 14, 19, 20, 22, 25, 26, 30, 31, 32, 33, 34, 39, 41, 42, 43, 49, and 52.

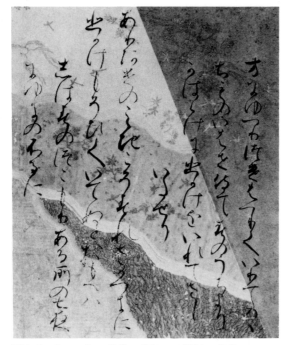

Right-hand page from *Collected Poems of Thirty-six Poets*.

SPECIAL OCCASIONS

*Add a little cheer to joyous times
or make a friend happy with these
wonderful wrapping ideas.*

Gifts for baby
see page 93, Gifts 44–47

Christmas gifts
see page 97, Gifts 48–53

Gifts for him
see page 104, Gifts 54–57

Gifts for baby

Babies themselves are rather like gifts to the world. These wrappings have some of the softness and light that babies bring with them.

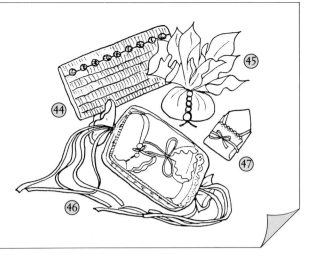

This beautiful rosebud package uses an Edo period (1600–1868) technique for making crepe paper. Creped *washi* was used in boxes containing art objects to protect them from damage.

Materials

GIFT
Box: ¾″ (h) × 9¾″ (w) × 4½″ (l)

PAPER
9″ × 18¾″ *lightweight pink* washi,
1 sheet, or 9 sheets of 3″ × 6¼″
lightweight pink washi
12½″ × 15¾″ *lightweight pink* washi

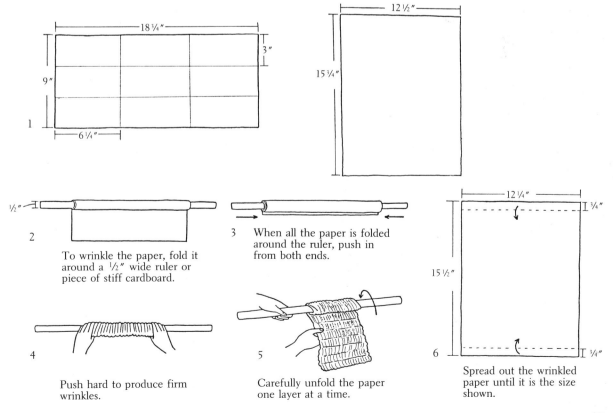

1   18¾″   3″   9″   6¼″

12½″   15¾″

2   ½″   To wrinkle the paper, fold it around a ½″ wide ruler or piece of stiff cardboard.

3   When all the paper is folded around the ruler, push in from both ends.

6   12¼″   1 ¾″   15½″   ¾″   Spread out the wrinkled paper until it is the size shown.

4   Push hard to produce firm wrinkles.

5   Carefully unfold the paper one layer at a time.

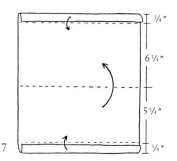

7

Fold in the top and bottom ¾" of the paper. Fold the edges over once again. Fold up the bottom half of the paper, leaving about a 1" gap between the folded edges.

11

When the paper is completely rolled, pinch and twist the thinner section for the stem.

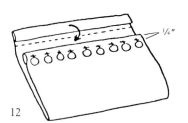

8

Place the gift inside and glue down the sides.

12

Staple or glue the rosebuds to the wrapping about ¼" from the edge.

9

To make the rosebuds, take each small sheet of paper and wrinkle it as in steps 2 to 4.

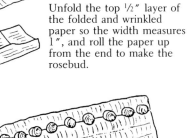

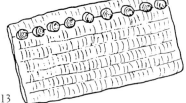

10

Unfold the top ½" layer of the folded and wrinkled paper so the width measures 1", and roll the paper up from the end to make the rosebud.

13

Fold down the upper flap so that it hides the staples. Secure with double-faced tape or glue. Bend each rosebud back toward the flap so the roses "stand up."

(45)

Because Japanese consider it rude to give a gift to even a small child without wrapping it, children's gifts were often placed on paper which was then gathered up and twisted closed in a technique called *o-hineri*.

Materials

GIFT
Baby shoes

PAPER
20" × 20" semi-transparent white paper with pink decorations

OTHER MATERIALS
6 strands of 25" long mizuhiki *made from crochet cotton (see page 68)*

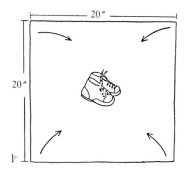

Place the shoes in the middle of the paper and lift the four corners of the paper up.

2

Gather the paper and tie it with the *mizuhiki* strands.

3

Cross the strand ends, and pass the upper end under and then over the other. Repeat to form five loops. Knot strands after the fifth loop to secure.

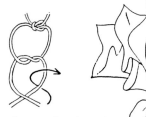

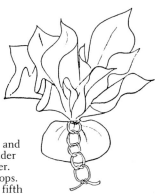

46

The silk gauze displays the baby clothes advantageously. The festive ribbon grouping at the ends makes the whole package look like a large piece of candy.

Materials

GIFT
2″(h)×6″(w)×9″(l) basket filled with baby clothes

PAPER
18″×20″ white silk gauze

OTHER MATERIALS
50″ of ½″ gauze ribbon, 2 strands of white and 2 strands of red
Small artificial flowers

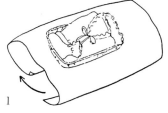

1

Arrange the gift items in the basket. Add a decorative sticker or try adding a rattle or a small stuffed toy. Place the gauze over and around the basket.

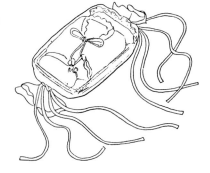

2

Gather the gauze together at the ends of the basket. Tie one end with the red ribbons and the other with the white ribbons. Here small artificial flowers have been sprinkled over the gauze.

47

This simple shape has been used for years in Japan to wrap money. The paper doily gives the gift a soft, clean feeling. Use this wrapping for gift soaps, handkerchiefs, or small baby toys. The pocket formed at the top can hold a little something extra—perhaps a card or a small flower.

Materials

GIFT
Box (or folded gift): 1″(h)×2¼″(w)×3″(l)

PAPER
9¾″×14½″ white lace doily

OTHER MATERIALS
18″ of ¼″ pink ribbon

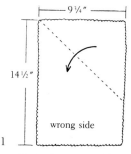

1

With the wrong side face up, fold down the upper right corner of the lace paper so that the top edge meets the left edge.

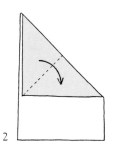

2

Fold down the upper left corner.

3

Unfold.

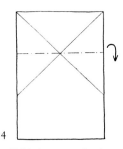

4

Fold the paper back and away, using the point where the diagonal folds intersect as your guide.

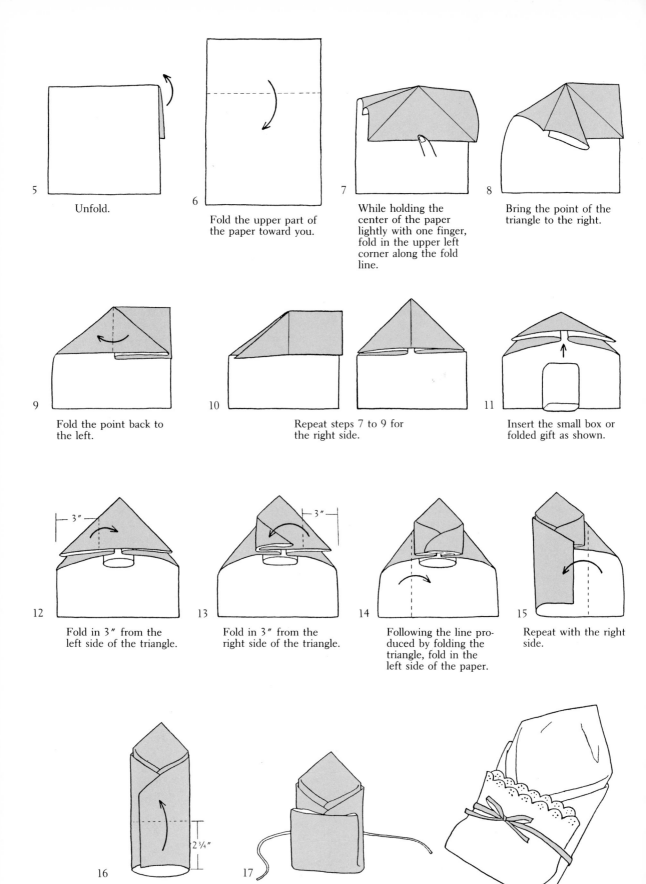

5 Unfold.

6 Fold the upper part of the paper toward you.

7 While holding the center of the paper lightly with one finger, fold in the upper left corner along the fold line.

8 Bring the point of the triangle to the right.

9 Fold the point back to the left.

10 Repeat steps 7 to 9 for the right side.

11 Insert the small box or folded gift as shown.

12 Fold in 3″ from the left side of the triangle.

13 Fold in 3″ from the right side of the triangle.

14 Following the line produced by folding the triangle, fold in the left side of the paper.

15 Repeat with the right side.

16 Fold up 2¾″ of the bottom of the wrapping.

17 Wrap with ribbon, and tie a bow at the front.

Christmas gifts

These festive wrappings are guaranteed to add enjoyment to your Christmas gift giving. Try using gold and silver in addition to the traditional red and green of Christmas.

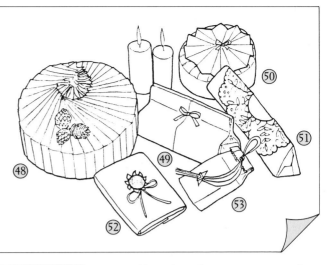

This golden pleated wrapping gives a fruit cake or a round of cheese an exciting new look. Gold pinecones complement the wrapping. Or try a piece of spruce on white paper or a sprig of holly on green paper to capture the same effect.

Materials

GIFT
Round box (or can): 4″ (h) × 8¾″ (d)

PAPER
13¾″ × 7′4½″ medium-weight gold paper

OTHER MATERIALS
3 pinecones (painted gold)
Double-faced tape
6″ of wire

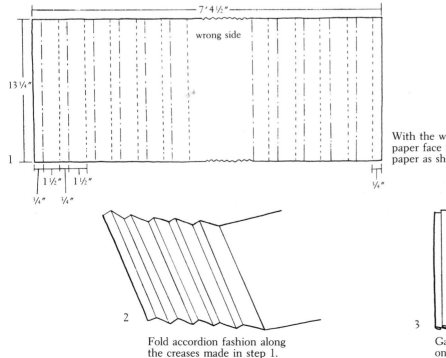

7′4½″

wrong side

13¾″

1

1½″ 1½″

¾″ ¾″

¾″

With the wrong side of the paper face up, crease the paper as shown.

2

Fold accordion fashion along the creases made in step 1.

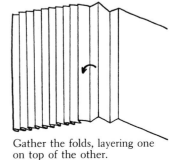

3

Gather the folds, layering one on top of the other.

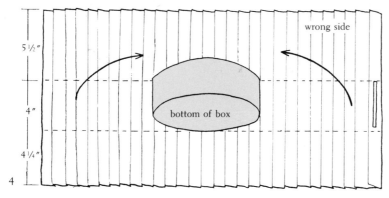

5½"

4"

4¼"

wrong side

bottom of box

4

With the wrong side of the paper face up, position the round box or gift on its side as shown. Put double-faced tape or glue on the right edge of the paper and wrap the paper around the gift.

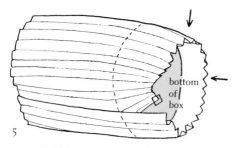

bottom of box

5

Fold the paper at the bottom in to the center, sliding the layers closer together in the center.

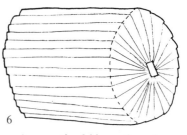

6

Arrange the folds neatly and tape at the bottom.

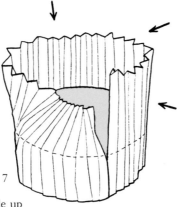

7

Turn the gift right side up and begin folding the paper down.

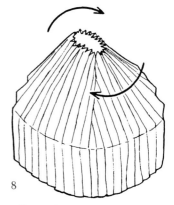

8

Shape the paper at the top by sliding the layers of folds into a spiral.

9

Wire the three pinecones together.

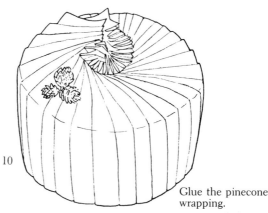

10

Glue the pinecones on the wrapping.

49

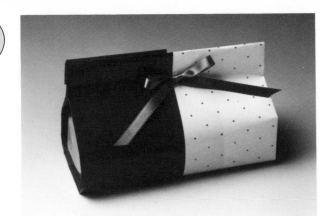

Wrap homemade banana bread or pound cake in festive Christmas colors. The tenting protects the top of the food.

Materials

GIFT
Cake or bread: 2½″(h) × 2½″(w) × 6¾″(l)

PAPER
9½″ × 14″ medium-weight white paper with gold polka dots
4¾″ × 14″ medium-weight red paper
6¾″ × ½″ cardboard

OTHER MATERIALS
13″ of ½″ green ribbon
Double-faced tape

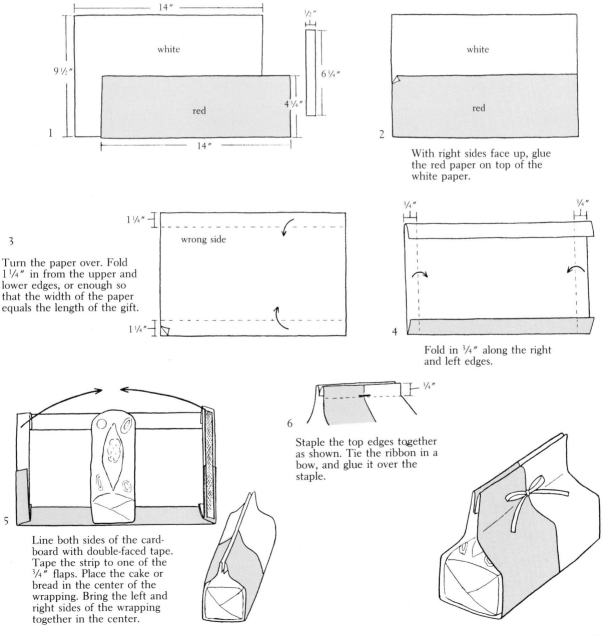

1

2
With right sides face up, glue the red paper on top of the white paper.

3
Turn the paper over. Fold 1¼″ in from the upper and lower edges, or enough so that the width of the paper equals the length of the gift.

4
Fold in ¾″ along the right and left edges.

5
Line both sides of the cardboard with double-faced tape. Tape the strip to one of the ¾″ flaps. Place the cake or bread in the center of the wrapping. Bring the left and right sides of the wrapping together in the center.

6
Staple the top edges together as shown. Tie the ribbon in a bow, and glue it over the staple.

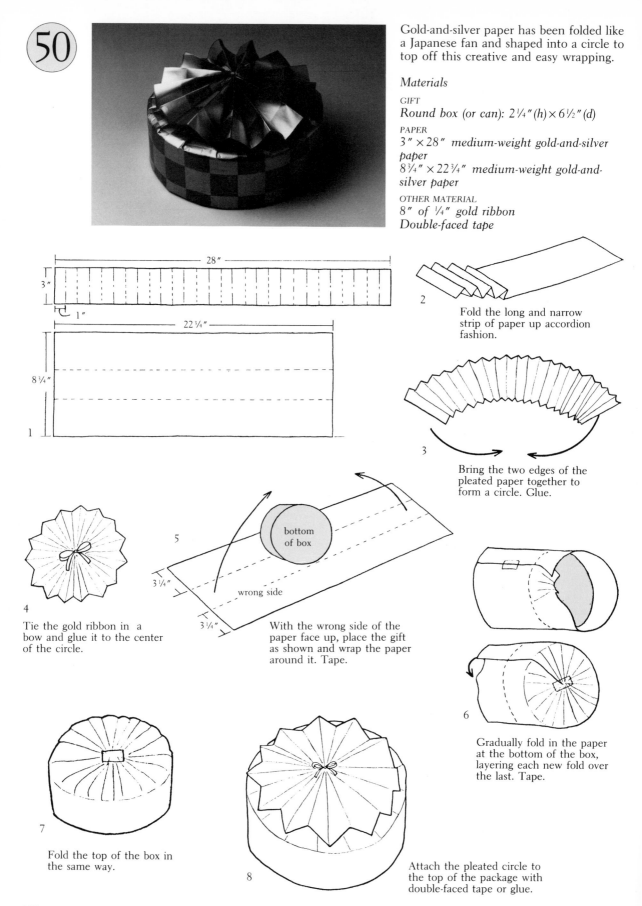

Gold-and-silver paper has been folded like a Japanese fan and shaped into a circle to top off this creative and easy wrapping.

Materials

GIFT
Round box (or can): 2¼″ (h) × 6½″ (d)

PAPER
3″ × 28″ medium-weight gold-and-silver paper
8¾″ × 22¾″ medium-weight gold-and-silver paper

OTHER MATERIAL
8″ of ¼″ gold ribbon
Double-faced tape

28″

3″

1″

22¾″

8¾″

1

2 Fold the long and narrow strip of paper up accordion fashion.

3 Bring the two edges of the pleated paper together to form a circle. Glue.

4 Tie the gold ribbon in a bow and glue it to the center of the circle.

5 bottom of box

wrong side

3¼″

3¼″

With the wrong side of the paper face up, place the gift as shown and wrap the paper around it. Tape.

6 Gradually fold in the paper at the bottom of the box, layering each new fold over the last. Tape.

7 Fold the top of the box in the same way.

8 Attach the pleated circle to the top of the package with double-faced tape or glue.

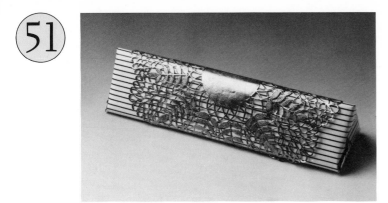

Adding a gold lace doily livens up this simple triangular box. A sticker or paper snowflake could be used instead of the doily.

Materials

GIFT
*Triangular box: 2½" (side of triangle)
× 9½" (l)*

PAPER
*8¼" × 11" medium-weight white-and-black striped paper
8" (d) gold paper doily*

To determine the proper size of paper for your box, see the instructions on page 32.

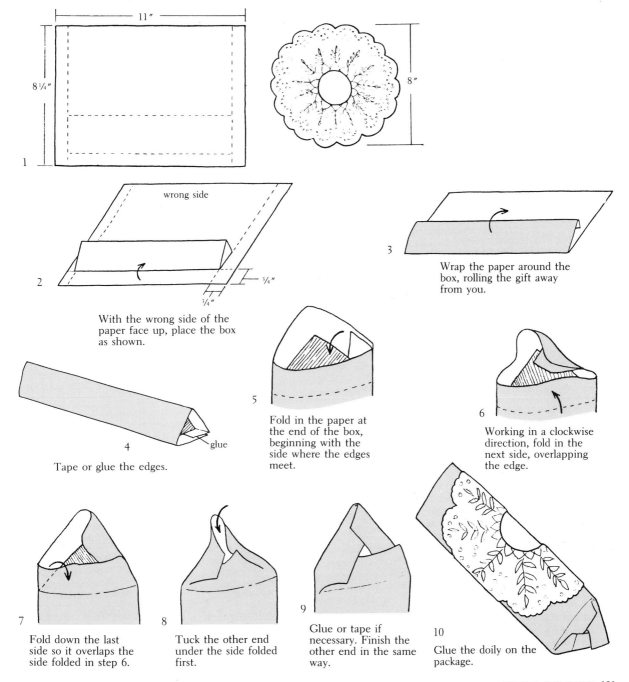

1

11"

8¼"

8"

2 — wrong side
¾"
¾"

With the wrong side of the paper face up, place the box as shown.

3 — Wrap the paper around the box, rolling the gift away from you.

4 — glue
Tape or glue the edges.

5 — Fold in the paper at the end of the box, beginning with the side where the edges meet.

6 — Working in a clockwise direction, fold in the next side, overlapping the edge.

7 — Fold down the last side so it overlaps the side folded in step 6.

8 — Tuck the other end under the side folded first.

9 — Glue or tape if necessary. Finish the other end in the same way.

10 — Glue the doily on the package.

52

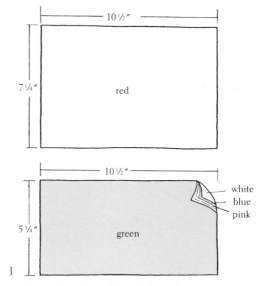

A flowerlike cut and the use of layering make a perky and attractive wrapping for this children's book. Change the shape of the cut and the gift underneath and this wrapping can be used for a surprising variety of gifts.

Materials

GIFT
Book: ½″ (thickness) × 4¼″ (w) × 5¾″ (l)

PAPER
7¼″ × 10½″ medium-weight red paper
5¾″ × 10½″ lightweight paper, 1 sheet each of white, blue, pink, and green

OTHER MATERIALS
18″ of gold cord

1 Layer the white, blue, pink, and green paper as shown, right sides up. Glue at the corners to prevent shifting.

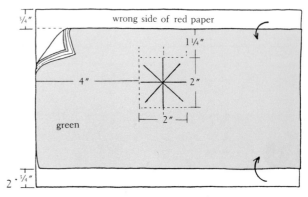

2 Glue the wrong side of the white bottom layer to the wrong side of the red paper as shown, and fold in ¾″ excess along the top and bottom edges. Cut slits in the paper where indicated.

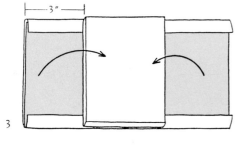

3 Place the book on the paper and fold up the paper on either side of it. Tape.

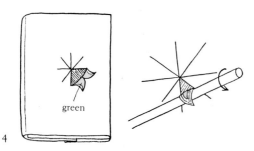

4 Turn the package over. Curl each petal of the flower with a pencil as shown.

5 Wrap the gold cord around the flower and tie a bow underneath.

53

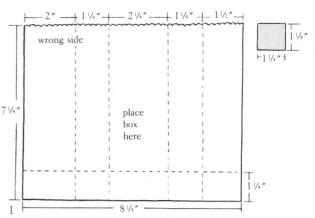

Trim the top of the paper with pinking shears, and score or mark the fold lines on the wrong side. Place the box as shown.

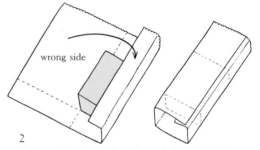

2

Fold up first the right side and then the left.

3

Finish the bottom: fold in the paper at the sides, bring up the bottom flap, and tape down the top flap.

The simplicity and versatility of this wrapping make it a natural for variations as shown on the back jacket of this book. The flowing curve of the *mizuhiki* is reminiscent of a bird in flight.

Materials

GIFT
Box: 1 1/4" (h) × 2 1/4" (w) × 3 1/2" (l)

PAPER
7 1/4" × 8 1/4" white paper flecked with gold
1 1/4" × 1 1/4" gold paper

OTHER MATERIALS
2 strands of 23" gold mizuhiki (see page 68)

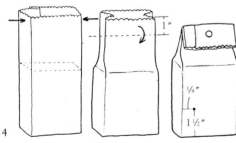

4

Stand the box upright. Push in the sides of the mouth of the bag. Fold down 1" of the top. Punch a hole in the middle of the folded area.

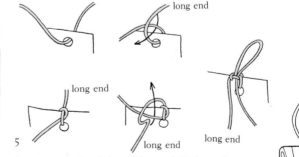

5

Pass the two strands of the gold *mizuhiki* through the hole, leaving 16" on the side closest to you. Pass the long end over and then under the short end, and tie loosely. Make a loop of the long end and pass the loop over and then under the short end.

7

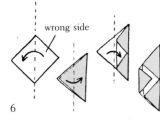

6

Fold the small gold square in half diagonally. Fold the point of the top layer over as shown. Fold the bottom layer over the first, so that the wrong side forms a decorative V.

Glue the gold paper over the loose ends of the gold *mizuhiki*, making a cranelike shape out of the gold *mizuhiki*.

Gifts for him

Common gifts for men like gloves, ties, and pens can be changed into uncommon gifts with these interesting and different wrappings. Vary the color and kind of paper to match his personality.

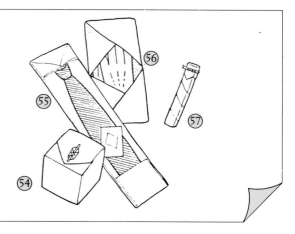

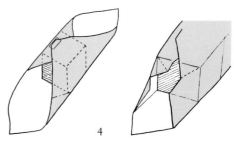

In this variant of wrapping on a diagonal (see Gifts 4 and 5), a cubic box placed in the middle of the paper produces an interesting final flap. A decorative *noshi* (see Gift 12) is an extra, thoughtful touch.

Materials

GIFT
Box: 3¾″ (h) × 3¾″ (w) × 3¾″ (l)
PAPER
13½″ × 13½″ medium-weight dark green paper
1½″ × 1½″ medium-weight red paper
¼″ × 3″ medium-weight white paper

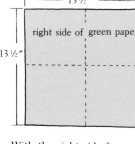

1
With the right side face up, fold the green paper into fourths. Crease and unfold.

2
Turn the paper over and mark or score as shown. Place the box in the center, aligning corners of the box with the folds made in step 1. Fold up the upper left and lower right corners.

3
Tape.

4
Fold in the paper at the end of the box, aligning the fold lines with the edges of the box and folding the excess paper inward. Small flaps of paper will peek out over the top of the box.

5
Bring the paper up completely, and fold it over the top of the box.

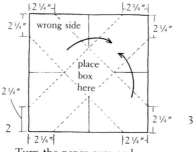

6
Repeat steps 4 and 5 with the other end.

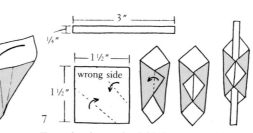

7
To make the *noshi*, fold the upper right and lower left corners of the red paper in on a slight slant as shown. Fold back where they overlap at the center. Thread a narrow strip of white paper through the center.

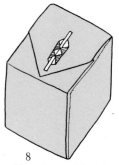

8
Glue the *noshi* to the package.

The upper strip of this package mimics a shirt collar, and the cellophane cover protects the tie while letting you see the design.

Materials

GIFT
Necktie

PAPER
4½″ × 26″ medium-weight brown kraft paper
14¾″ × 23¾″ cellophane

OTHER MATERIALS
Card or note (optional)

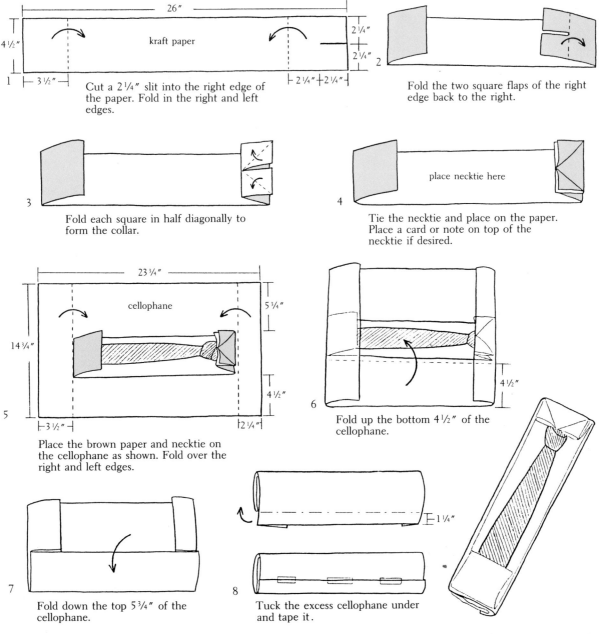

1. Cut a 2¼″ slit into the right edge of the paper. Fold in the right and left edges.

2. Fold the two square flaps of the right edge back to the right.

3. Fold each square in half diagonally to form the collar.

4. Tie the necktie and place on the paper. Place a card or note on top of the necktie if desired.

5. Place the brown paper and necktie on the cellophane as shown. Fold over the right and left edges.

6. Fold up the bottom 4½″ of the cellophane.

7. Fold down the top 5¾″ of the cellophane.

8. Tuck the excess cellophane under and tape it.

This sleek wrapping is really nothing more than two cleverly folded chopstick holders fitted together. The length can be adjusted slightly to the size of the gift. Try wrapping a handkerchief or wallet.

Materials

GIFT
Men's leather gloves (maximum size):
5½" × 8"

PAPER
22" × 26¼" medium-weight white-and-black checked paper, 2 sheets
5½" × 8" medium-weight black shiny paper

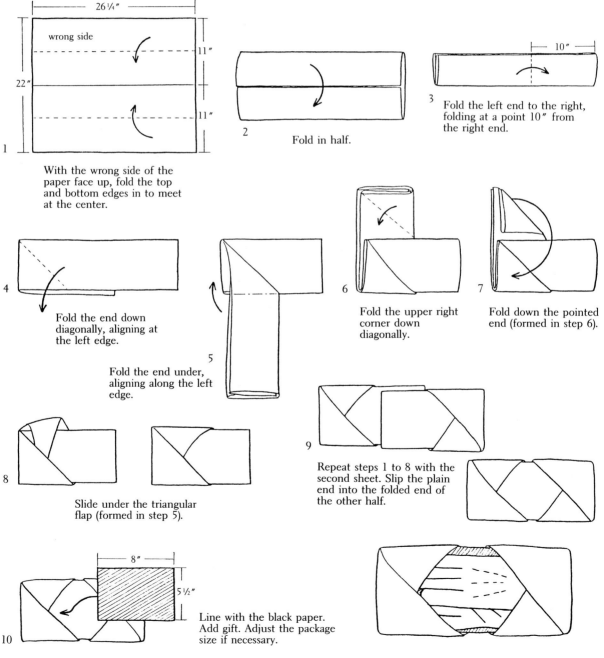

1 With the wrong side of the paper face up, fold the top and bottom edges in to meet at the center.

2 Fold in half.

3 Fold the left end to the right, folding at a point 10" from the right end.

4 Fold the end down diagonally, aligning at the left edge.

5 Fold the end under, aligning along the left edge.

6 Fold the upper right corner down diagonally.

7 Fold down the pointed end (formed in step 6).

8 Slide under the triangular flap (formed in step 5).

9 Repeat steps 1 to 8 with the second sheet. Slip the plain end into the folded end of the other half.

10 Line with the black paper. Add gift. Adjust the package size if necessary.

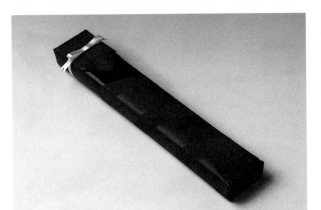

In this technique, the wrapping is wound around the box at an angle. This angularity is repeated in the shape of the cap. Perfect for a pen or paper knife.

Materials

GIFT
Box: ¾″(h)×1½″(w)×9″(l)
PAPER
2¾″×14¼″ medium-weight wine red paper
4″×4″ medium-weight wine red paper
OTHER MATERIALS
5″ of ¼″ silver-gray ribbon
7″ of ¼″ silver-gray ribbon

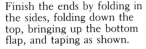

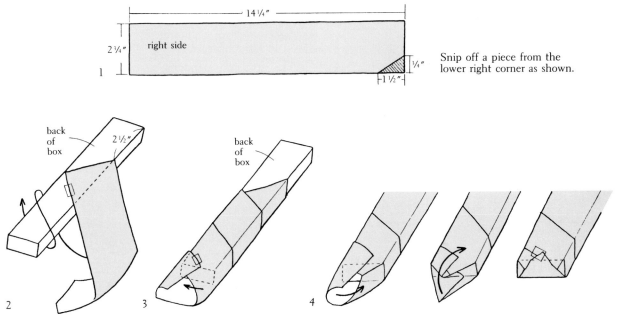

1   Snip off a piece from the lower right corner as shown.

2   Position the paper as shown on the back of the box. Tape it in place and wind the paper around the box.

3   Tape the end of the paper.

4   Finish the ends by folding in the sides, folding down the top, bringing up the bottom flap, and taping as shown.

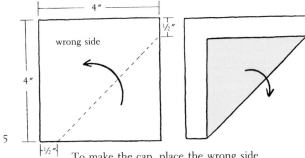

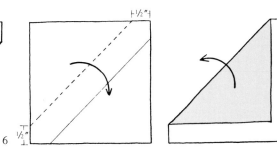

5   To make the cap, place the wrong side of the 4″ square face up, then fold up the lower right corner and crease the paper along the dotted line. Unfold.

6   Fold down the upper left corner and unfold.

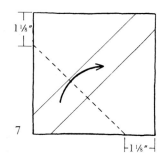

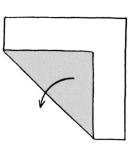

7

Fold up the lower left corner and unfold.

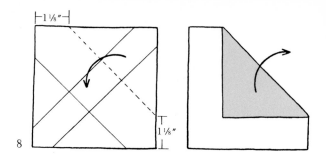

8

Fold down the upper right corner and unfold.

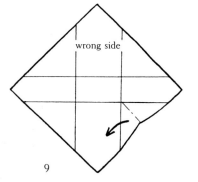

wrong side

9

Position the paper as shown. Using the line as a guide, fold in the lower right side.

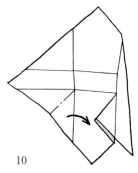

10

Fold in the lower left side.

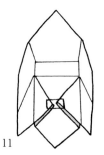

11

Tape the paper in the middle.

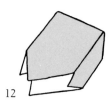

12

Repeat with the upper left and right sides.

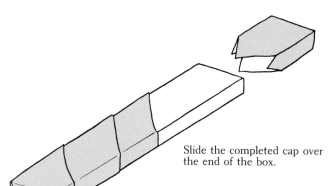

13

Slide the completed cap over the end of the box.

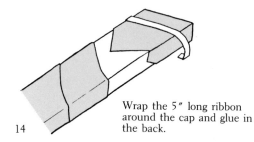

14

Wrap the 5″ long ribbon around the cap and glue in the back.

15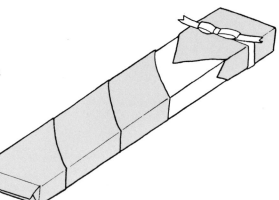

Tie the 7″ long ribbon in a bow and glue it on to the ribbon.

FUROSHIKI

These traditional furoshiki wrappings are versatile, practical, and incredibly easy.

Basic and simple
see page 114, Gift 58

Variations
see page 115, Gifts 59–63

Bottles and balls
see page 119, Gifts 64–66

Basic and simple

A box is easy for beginners to wrap, but adaptable furoshiki can wrap gifts of varied shapes and sizes. The technique of wrapping with a furoshiki resembles that of wrapping boxes at a slant.

(58)

Furoshiki

A furoshiki *is a square piece of material used to wrap and carry objects of all shapes and sizes. Its corners are drawn up and knotted into a makeshift handle. The etymology of the word* furoshiki *helps us understand how the custom began:* furo *means bath, and* shiki *means rug or mat, thus a* furoshiki *was originally a type of bath mat. Early Japanese baths were similar to steam baths, and at bath time one wore a lightweight, white cotton kimono. The bather spread out a* furoshiki *and stood on it while he undressed. He changed into the white kimono and wrapped the* furoshiki *around the clothes he had taken off. After his bath, the bather dressed standing on the* furoshiki *and wrapped his damp white kimono in it to carry home from the bath. This early bath mat developed into the modern* furoshiki, *a multi-purpose carryall.*

The word furoshiki *probably came into use sometime between 1688 and 1710, but Japanese people were wrap-*

A woman peddler carries her wares in a *furoshiki* in this Edo period print by Utamaro.

ping their belongings in square pieces of cloth much earlier; scrolls from the Kamakura (1185–1333) and Muromachi (1336–1573) periods show women carrying bundles of clothing on their heads. Originally furoshiki *were made from whatever material was available—it was simply cut to an appropriate shape. About the middle of the Edo period (1603–1867), however, specially made* furoshiki *bearing family crests or shop insignia began to gain popularity. These were generally died a deep indigo.*

Today, furoshiki *are made from cotton, silk, or blends and range in size from squares of fourteen and a half inches to seven feet eight inches—the latter being large enough to wrap Japanese bedding. In general, the most common sizes are twenty-one and a half inches, twenty-seven and a half inches, twenty-nine and a half inches, and thirty-five and a half inches.*

Early furoshiki *were not, in fact, always perfectly square. Any material on hand was likely to be pressed into service as a* furoshiki, *and squareness was not a necessary prerequisite. The ease with which the material could be tied was more important, and thus thicker materials were avoided in favor of soft, strong ones—cotton being the most common. Now* furoshiki *are produced commercially and are usually perfect squares. You can easily make your own by cutting a square of cloth, folding under the edges, and stitching. Large handkerchiefs, bandannas, or scarves can be substituted as well.*

The convenience of the furoshiki *lies in its adaptability. It has no definite shape as does a bag, and wrapping at a slant makes use of the stretchy bias of the fabric, making it possible to stretch the cloth to accommodate the object by simply pulling on the corners. The* furoshiki *can adapt to fit whatever you put in it and is equally suitable for wrapping small and large objects, round or square ones, and even irregularly shaped ones. The* furoshiki *wrapping prevents the contents from shifting around and even odd-shaped packages can be carried quite easily.*

In addition to being convenient, furoshiki *can be expressive: enhance a gift by choosing appropriate materials, colors, patterns, sizes, and knots for tying the* furoshiki. *Let the softness of cloth (as opposed to the stiffness of paper) open up new and exciting possibilities.*

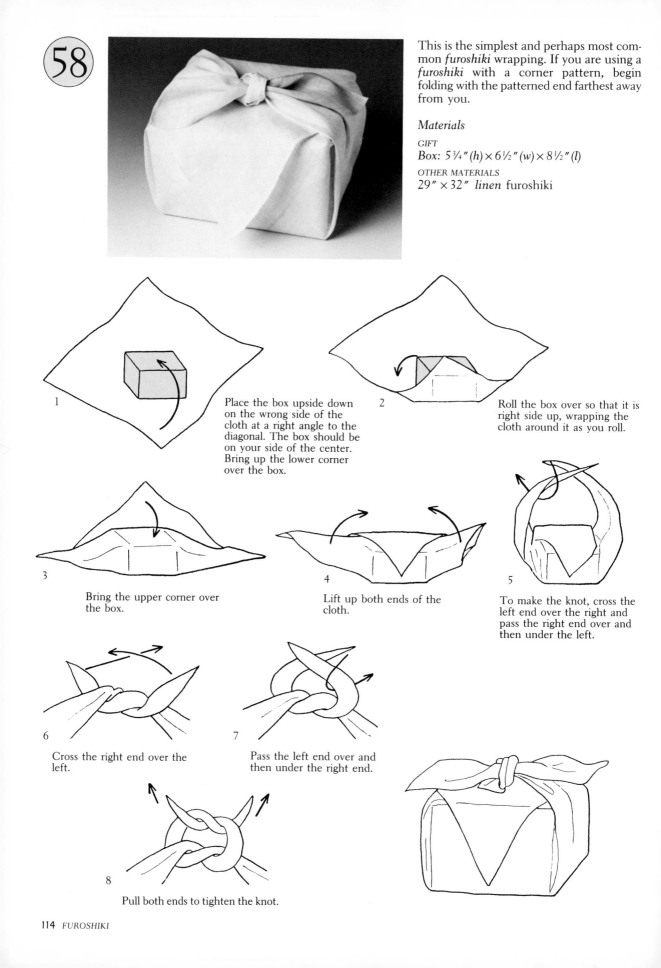

58

This is the simplest and perhaps most common *furoshiki* wrapping. If you are using a *furoshiki* with a corner pattern, begin folding with the patterned end farthest away from you.

Materials

GIFT
Box: 5 ¾″ (h) × 6 ½″ (w) × 8 ½″ (l)
OTHER MATERIALS
29″ × 32″ *linen* furoshiki

1 Place the box upside down on the wrong side of the cloth at a right angle to the diagonal. The box should be on your side of the center. Bring up the lower corner over the box.

2 Roll the box over so that it is right side up, wrapping the cloth around it as you roll.

3 Bring the upper corner over the box.

4 Lift up both ends of the cloth.

5 To make the knot, cross the left end over the right and pass the right end over and then under the left.

6 Cross the right end over the left.

7 Pass the left end over and then under the right end.

8 Pull both ends to tighten the knot.

Variations

While the technique of wrapping on the diagonal remains constant, there are many ways to wrap and tie furoshiki *depending on the size and shape of the gift to be wrapped.*

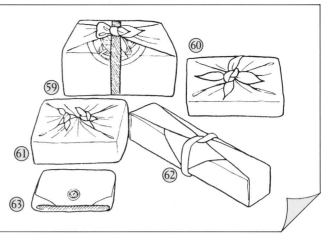

The addition of a ribbon around the center of the *furoshiki* prevents the wrapping from slipping and makes larger packages easy to manage.

Materials

GIFT
Box: 4″(h) × 7½″(w) × 10″(l)

OTHER MATERIALS
28½″ × 31½″ *silk* furoshiki
38″ *of* ¾″ *ribbon*

1 Place the box at a 90° angle to the diagonal of the cloth and closer to the lower corner. Bring up the lower corner over the box.

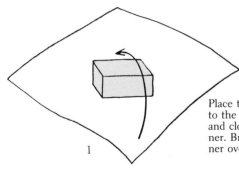

2 Bring the upper corner of the cloth over the box.

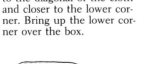

3 Tuck the excess cloth under the box.

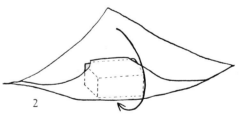

4 Tie the ribbon around the center of the box, knotting at the side. Lift both ends of the cloth. Turn the box around.

5 Cross the left end over the right and tie once. Make a loop of the right end and cross it over the left.

6 Pass the left end over and then under the loop.

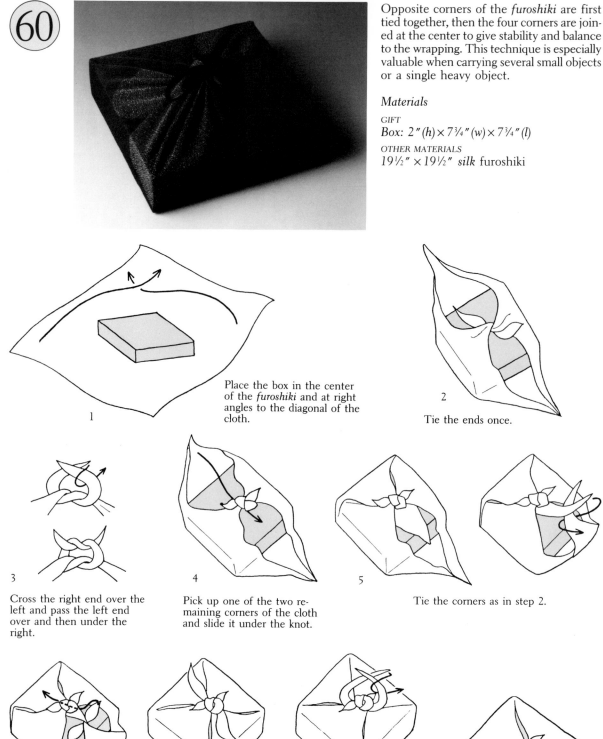

60

Opposite corners of the *furoshiki* are first tied together, then the four corners are joined at the center to give stability and balance to the wrapping. This technique is especially valuable when carrying several small objects or a single heavy object.

Materials

GIFT
Box: 2″(h) × 7¾″(w) × 7¾″(l)
OTHER MATERIALS
19½″ × 19½″ silk furoshiki

1

Place the box in the center of the *furoshiki* and at right angles to the diagonal of the cloth.

2

Tie the ends once.

3

Cross the right end over the left and pass the left end over and then under the right.

4

Pick up one of the two remaining corners of the cloth and slide it under the knot.

5

Tie the corners as in step 2.

6

Slide the new knot under the old knot.

7

Tie the ends of the new knot over the old knot following step 3.

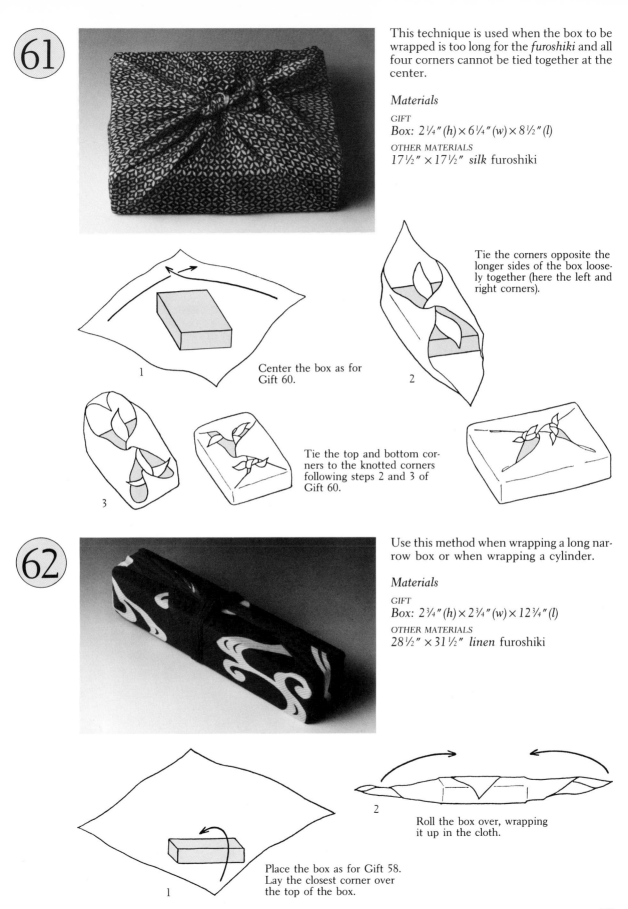

61

This technique is used when the box to be wrapped is too long for the *furoshiki* and all four corners cannot be tied together at the center.

Materials

GIFT
Box: $2\frac{1}{4}''(h) \times 6\frac{1}{4}''(w) \times 8\frac{1}{2}''(l)$

OTHER MATERIALS
$17\frac{1}{2}'' \times 17\frac{1}{2}''$ *silk* furoshiki

1   Center the box as for Gift 60.

Tie the corners opposite the longer sides of the box loosely together (here the left and right corners).

2

3

Tie the top and bottom corners to the knotted corners following steps 2 and 3 of Gift 60.

62

Use this method when wrapping a long narrow box or when wrapping a cylinder.

Materials

GIFT
Box: $2\frac{3}{4}''(h) \times 2\frac{3}{4}''(w) \times 12\frac{3}{4}''(l)$

OTHER MATERIALS
$28\frac{1}{2}'' \times 31\frac{1}{2}''$ *linen* furoshiki

2   Roll the box over, wrapping it up in the cloth.

1   Place the box as for Gift 58. Lay the closest corner over the top of the box.

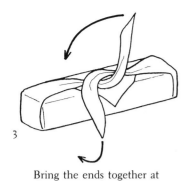

3

Bring the ends together at
the center and cross.

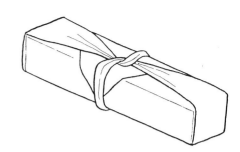

4

Pass the ends under the box
and tie them securely as in
steps 2 and 3 of Gift 60.

(63)

This technique is thought to be the most
refined and most formal of the *furoshiki*
wrappings. It is also the only one with no
knots and can come unwrapped rather
easily.

Materials

GIFT
*½″(h) × 3½″(w) × 5¾″(l) rectangular flat
item (photograph in paper frame)*
OTHER MATERIALS
11¾″ × 11¾″ silk furoshiki

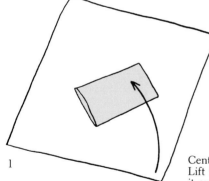

1

Center the gift as for Gift 60.
Lift the lower corner and lay
it over the gift.

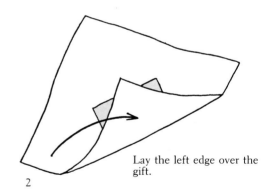

2

Lay the left edge over the
gift.

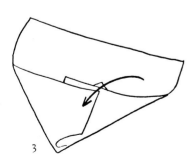

3

Lay the right edge over
the gift.

4

Fold down the upper flap
over the gift.

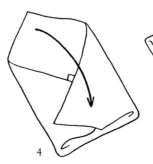

5

Tuck the excess cloth
into the fold.

Bottles and balls

The versatile and practical furoshiki *makes a strong, flexible, and easily carried wrapping for irregular shapes such as bottles and balls.*

You can carry this fast and easy wrapping by the knot formed at the top.

Materials

GIFT
12″(h) bottle of wine
OTHER MATERIALS
29½″ × 29½″ silk furoshiki

1

Place the bottle in the center of the cloth. Bring the top and bottom corners of the cloth over the top of the bottle and tie as in steps 2 and 3 of Gift 60.

2

Cross the remaining two corners in front of the bottle.

3

Wrap the corners around the bottle.

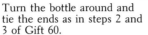

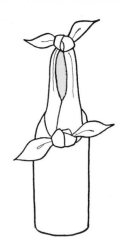

4

 Turn the bottle around and
tie the ends as in steps 2 and
3 of Gift 60.

65

Just as easy to do and carry as Gift 64, this
technique wraps two bottles separately in
the same square of cloth.

Materials

GIFT
12"(h) bottle of wine, 2 bottles
OTHER MATERIALS
33" × 33" cotton furoshiki

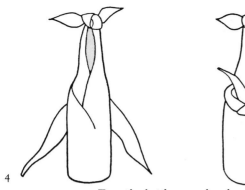

1

Place the two bottles as
shown on the diagonal of the
cloth. The space between the
bottoms of the bottles must
be slightly more than twice
the diameter of the bottles.
Roll the bottles up in the
cloth.

2

Stand the bottles up.

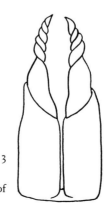

3

Twist the ends of the cloth
and tie as in steps 2 and 3 of
Gift 60.

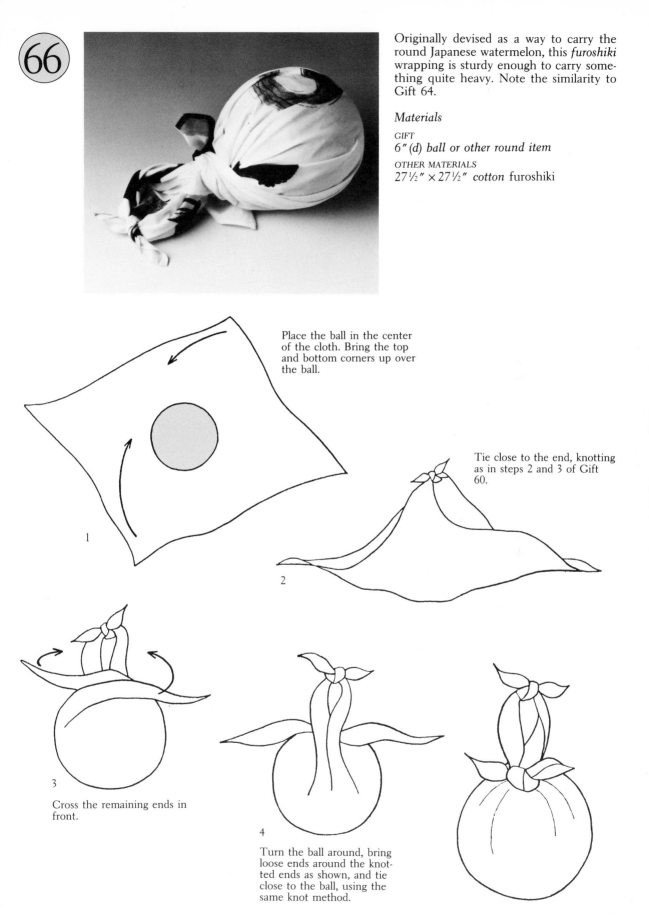

66

Originally devised as a way to carry the round Japanese watermelon, this *furoshiki* wrapping is sturdy enough to carry something quite heavy. Note the similarity to Gift 64.

Materials

GIFT
6″ (d) ball or other round item

OTHER MATERIALS
27½″ × 27½″ cotton furoshiki

Place the ball in the center of the cloth. Bring the top and bottom corners up over the ball.

1

Tie close to the end, knotting as in steps 2 and 3 of Gift 60.

2

3

Cross the remaining ends in front.

4

Turn the ball around, bring loose ends around the knotted ends as shown, and tie close to the ball, using the same knot method.

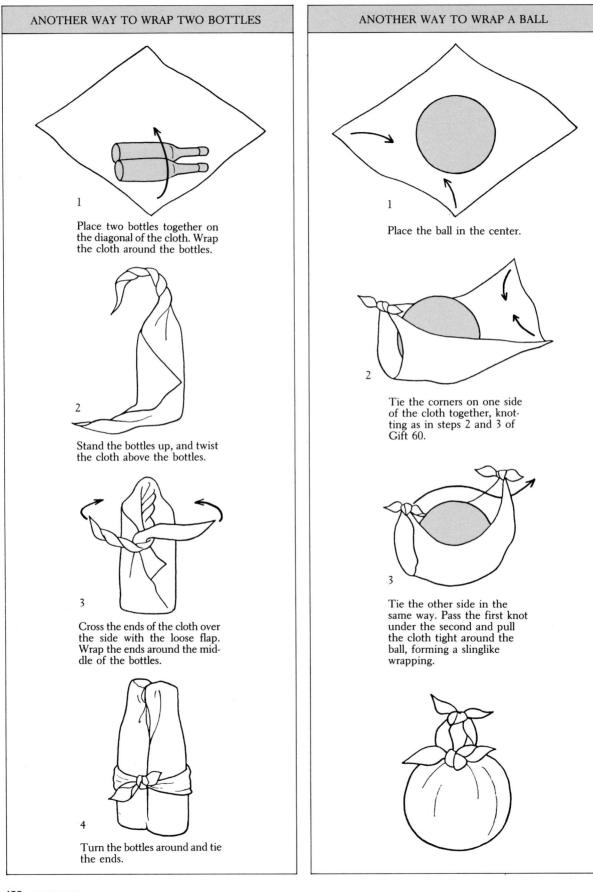

ANOTHER WAY TO WRAP TWO BOTTLES

1

Place two bottles together on the diagonal of the cloth. Wrap the cloth around the bottles.

2

Stand the bottles up, and twist the cloth above the bottles.

3

Cross the ends of the cloth over the side with the loose flap. Wrap the ends around the middle of the bottles.

4

Turn the bottles around and tie the ends.

ANOTHER WAY TO WRAP A BALL

1

Place the ball in the center.

2

Tie the corners on one side of the cloth together, knotting as in steps 2 and 3 of Gift 60.

3

Tie the other side in the same way. Pass the first knot under the second and pull the cloth tight around the ball, forming a slinglike wrapping.

Appendix

WHERE TO BUY *WASHI*

Washi is available at large art supply stores and oriental import stores. The following shops are a partial listing.

SAM FLAX
15 Park Row, New York, New York 10038
(212) 620-3030
12 W. 20th St., New York, New York 10011
(212) 620-3038
25 E. 28th St., New York, New York 10016
(212) 620-3040
747 3rd Ave., New York, New York 10017
(212) 620-3050
55 E. 55th St., New York, New York 10022
(212) 620-3060
GENERAL INFORMATION
111 8th Ave., New York, New York 10011
(212) 620-3000

ZEN ORIENTAL
521 5th Ave., New York, New York 10017
(212) 697-0840
115 W. 57th St., New York, New York 10019
(212) 582-4622

KABUKI GIFTS AND IMPORTS
11355 Santa Monica Blvd., W. Los Angeles, California 90025

UWAJIMAYA
6th South and South King, Seattle, Washington 98104
(206) 624-6248

LEE'S ART SHOP
220 W. 57th St., New York, New York
(212) 247-0110

BUNKA-DO
340 E. 1st St., Los Angeles, California 90012
(213) 625-8673

KINOKUNIYA, SAN FRANCISCO
1581 Webster St., San Francisco, California 94115
(415) 567-7625

WHERE TO BUY ORIENTAL PAPERS

Oriental type papers may be substitued for *washi* to create a similar effect. The following oriental import stores and art supply stores are a partial listing.

KINOKUNIYA, LOS ANGELES
New Otani Hotel Arcade, 110 S. Los Angeles St., Los Angeles, California 90012
(213) 687-4447

NEW YORK CENTRAL ART SUPPLY
62 3rd Ave., New York, New York 10003
(212) 473-7705

PARSON ART SUPPLY
70 5th Ave., New York, New York 10011
(212) 675-6406

TORCH JOS
36 W. 15th St., New York, New York 10011
(212) 243-3534

KAREL ASSOCIATES, INC.
190 Henry, Stamford, Connecticut 06902
(NYC) (212) 725-0355

ANDREWS/NELSON/WHITEHEAD
31-10 48th Ave., Long Island City, New York
(718) 937-7100

WHERE TO BUY *MIZUHIKI*

Mizuhiki are available at oriental import stores like the ones below.

ZEN ORIENTAL
521 5th Ave., New York, New York 10017
(212) 697-0840
115 W. 57th St., New York, New York 10019
(212) 582-4622

BUNKA-DO
340 E. 1st St., Los Angeles, California 90012
(213) 625-8673

UWAJIMAYA
6th South and South King, Seattle, Washington 98104
(206) 624-6248

WHERE TO BUY GIFT WRAP AND RIBBON

Gift wrap and ribbon are available at card shops and department stores. Or contact the following stores for the address of a store close to your own home.

HALLMARK CARDS
MAIN OFFICE
25th and McGee, Kansas City, Missouri 64141

DENNISON PARTY BAZAAR
390 5th Ave., New York, New York 10018

WHERE TO BUY GESSO

Gesso is available at most art supply stores including those listed below.

SAM FLAX (Liquitex—acrylic gesso)
  15 Park Row, New York, New York 10038
    (212) 620-3030
  12 W. 20th St., New York, New York 10011
    (212) 620-3038
  25 E. 28th St., New York, New York 10016
    (212) 620-3040
  747 3rd Ave., New York, New York 10017
    (212) 620-3050
  55 E. 55th St., New York, New York 10022
    (212) 620-3060
  GENERAL INFORMATION
      111 8th Ave., New York, New York 10011
      (212) 620-3000

PEARL PAINT CO, INC. (Liquitex—acrylic gesso)
  380 Canal St., New York, New York 10013
  1033 E. Oakland Park Blvd., Fort Lauderdale,
    Florida 33334
  2411 Hempstead Turnpike, East Meadow,
    New York 11554
  MAIL ORDER
    (212) 431-7932

NEW YORK CENTRAL ART SUPPLY
62 3rd Ave., New York, New York 10003
  (212) 473-7705

LEE'S ART SHOP
220 W. 57th St., New York, New York 10019
  (212) 247-0110